A Taste of Heaven

First steps for Jubilee 2000

Isabel Carter

Onwards and Upwards Publishers

3 Radfords Turf, Cranbrook, Exeter,
EX5 7DX, United Kingdom.
www.onwardsandupwards.org

This first edition published in the United Kingdom by Onwards and Upwards Publishers (2018).

ISBN:	978-1-78815-651-6
Typeface:	Sabon LT
Graphic design:	LM Graphic Design

Photography:	Tearfund, Richard Hanson	pp. 14, 107, 131, 132, 159, back cover
	Mike Webb	p. 90, front cover
	Wingfinger Graphics	pp. 101, 157
	Claire Shelley	p. 124
	Keith Ellis	p. 137
	Jenny Matthews	p. 54
	Jubilee 2000	

Printed in the United Kingdom.

About the Author

Isabel Carter studied environmental and plant sciences in London University. She gained experience working first in Ethiopia and then in Papua New Guinea, focusing on crop agriculture. After a few years in editing agricultural publications, she worked with Tearfund for over 20 years, firstly working with farmers in a semi-arid area of Kenya, then as Editor of *Footsteps* and in later years coordinating their international publications. A passion for sharing and communicating information led to research into the flow of information among farmers, leading to a doctorate at Leeds University. Enabling the sharing of practical information in local languages became a particular focus in the latter years with Tearfund as a result of this research. She was a co-founder of Jubilee 2000.

In recent years her concerns have focused on raising awareness of lifestyle change and awareness regarding climate change, and enjoying voluntary work with nature conservation, practical work outdoors with school children, and bird watching and surveying.

Endorsements

If ever there were a modern example of the Kingdom of God beginning life as a seed, here it is! Isabel Carter was in the seed of Jubilee 2000. With great authority and passion, she traces its beginnings and shows how the seed was sown and germinated, growing shoots of freedom and fairness, justice and jubilee. It's a classic exposition of how great ideas and movements start from the bottom up and from small beginnings. An inspiration!

Formerly Bishop of Hull and Bishop of Liverpool,
the Rt Revd James Jones KBE ('for services to the bereaved and to justice')

This is a truly remarkable story: how one woman's vision and determination helped to change the world. The echoes of William Wilberforce were heard again as ordinary people demanded that the chains should be broken and people set free. The Jubilee trumpet was heard across the globe; by the world's most powerful leaders and the world's oppressed poor. I discovered – and thousands more like me – that my voice could be raised and it could make a difference. As a consequence, Tearfund – and many other charities – embraced advocacy and campaigning as an integral and essential component of their work. As the closing report of Jubilee 2000 said, "The world will never be the same." That's why I'm so delighted and grateful that Isabel has written this book: the perseverance, the battles, the characters, the setbacks and the bottlenecks are all there – and so are the inspirations, the encouragements and the breakthroughs. What a story... what a result!

Stephen Rand was Communications Director, then Prayer and Campaigns
Director for Tearfund; Jubilee 2000 Board Member, then Co-chair of
Jubilee Debt Campaign. He now works part-time for the APPG for
International Freedom of Religion or Belief and is Advocacy Consultant to
Open Doors UK&I

The international Jubilee 2000 campaign was transformative – not just of creditor-debtor relations across low income countries but for many organisations and individuals. Isabel Carter's deep faith played a critical role in the founding of Jubilee 2000 and its later success – which is why her story – this book – is an important contribution to an understanding of a global 'grass roots' campaign's achievements in challenging powerful vested financial interests.

Ann Pettifor, political economist and author.
Former Director of Jubilee 2000 Coalition UK
and now Director of Policy Research in Macroeconomics (PRIME)

Dedicated to all the wonderful individuals around the world
who 'caught' the vision of Jubilee 2000
and who brought the campaign into such vibrant life.

I hope this brings reminders of what was achieved together
and may inspire a few more 'nobodies' into action.

Contents

A Taste of Heaven

Prologue

...Jubilee 2000 has been comfortably the most successful mass movement of the past 25 years.

Larry Elliot, Guardian, November 2000

It's well over 20 years since I first became involved in the initial seeds of what was to grow into Jubilee 2000, an international coalition campaigning to cancel Third World debt as a one-off celebration of the millennium.

In the earlier years, my somewhat unusual entry point was kept quiet. Though well-known to all those closely involved at the time, it was felt it might prove an unhelpful media distraction to our core aims if it became widely known. It also suited me just fine to play a supportive role!

As the years have passed, I have occasional exchanges with puzzled Ph.D. students who try and add everything together and feel there is something missing in the public-facing accounts of its origins. I was happy for this part of the story to be ignored. But I find it fascinating how Jubilee 2000 is still referred to as such a successful campaign – indeed I have probably heard more references to it in recent years than ever, by groups working on climate change. So interest has not waned and an explanation of the very first, fragile years of the campaign may prove both of historic interest but also of current relevance. My personal story largely concludes as the highly effective coalition that took forward Jubilee 2000 swung into action – and the busy years between 1998 (which included the epic Birmingham G8 summit in May 1998) and 2000 are well recorded and documented. Yet with the deaths in 2014 of two of the other founder members, I am also aware that I now hold the only full documentation of these first early years when the campaign was shaped, focused and polished; years which helped ensure its lasting impact. Time to dust off the files, maybe, and stir up my memories.

In 2014, co-founder members Bill Peters and Martin Dent both died, after living to ripe old ages. Their jointly written book, *The Crisis of*

Poverty and Debt in the Third World, 1999[1] has long been in the public domain. But there is another side of the story that still needs to be told. Recuperating after two operations in quick succession provided the space for me to start writing.

Why me? Why was I specifically called to be involved? This was a question I never stopped asking at the time. But over time those reasons have clarified somewhat. God seeks out specific people for specific roles at opportune moments in time. God is still very much at work in our troubled world, still using the 'nobodies' of this world to achieve some surprising interventions. Ignoring his prompting is a well-practised skill that we would all do well to unlearn.

> *Martin Dent first had the idea of linking debt relief to the concept of Jubilee and the new millennium, back in 1990. ... Martin Dent and his friend Bill Peters tried for some time ... to persuade others of the value of their idea. To no avail ...*
>
> *One busy, hectic day, Martin asked if I would meet a friend of his, Isabel Carter. Reluctantly I fitted her in. As she sat down, she explained that she had had a vision. I groaned inside; thought, "Do I need this?" and tried not to show my scepticism. In her vision, she explained, God had called on her to work for Jubilee 2000. ... She came across Martin Dent and his friend Bill Peters. Now she had come to ask what she could do.*
>
> *Now a few months went by and she returned. She had obtained charitable status for a Jubilee 2000 campaign, and had found some money – a large sum of money! I began to take Isabel Carter very seriously.*
>
> *Ann Pettifor*
> *International Director of the Jubilee 2000 campaign*
> *These recollections are from a talk given to SEDOS, 17th February 1998*
>
> *Jubilee 2000 promoted change through solidarity – not through charity. The millennium link gave the idea an urgency and resonance. It was described as "an idea whose time had*

---

[1] ISBN 9780754610274

come". Previous debt campaigns had proved somewhat academic and too complex for supporters to mobilise behind, but Jubilee 2000 had a clear and simple focus, changing it from a complex issue of international debt and debt sustainability ratios, into one of justice with clear actions for supporters to engage with. Anyone who had borrowed money could understand about debt forgiveness.

Professor Margorie Mayo

CHAPTER ONE

The Human Chain in Birmingham

The Birmingham Chain

It all began in the Trowell services on the M1. I was in the toilets washing my hands, when a lady nearby caught my eye. Was her red T-shirt a coincidence? As I left the toilets, another two ladies came in with red jeans and sweatshirts. Were they also heading towards Birmingham? We shared a tentative smile. I felt a sense of anticipation. What kind of impact would this day have? Had news really spread that far?

Our coach party of 60 people had left the small East Riding town of South Cave, near Hull, at 7am that Saturday morning, May 16th, 1998. Our ages ranged from baby John at 8 months to Peter in his late 80s. We were a positive and friendly bunch, many of us either from the local church or part of the town's World Development Group. A few others had come and joined us from Llanidloes with my sister and family, squeezing into beds and floor space in our home the night before. The weather for the day's event in Birmingham looked good and it was great to have a whole day to enjoy each other's company. None of us knew quite how the day would unfold, but the planning and information had been good and we were all focused and informed. There was a variety of talks and events to take part in once we arrived in Birmingham to join the 'people's summit'. The message had been to "make a chain to break the chains of debt".

As our coach driver followed his route to first drop us off and then find his allocated parking, it became apparent that there really were a lot of coaches arriving. As we climbed down from the coach, it was clear that thousands of others were also disembarking. Indeed, the area was full of relaxed crowds of people, most sporting red clothing. This was really going to be big – so many thousands of people converging to make the day a success. As I looked around in a daze and fully realized the scale of what was to unfold, I burst into tears. I was simply overwhelmed by the scale of it; aware of the effort that so many people had made to come and support the day. For me it revealed the spread and flowering of an idea that had been given to me as a barely incomprehensible vision just a few years earlier. There had been many times during those years when I had questioned God, questioned my own role, questioned whether what we were trying to do could possibly be achievable. Now I was sure. This had all been worthwhile. God was indeed at work and 70,000 people in the UK were mobilised here in Birmingham, ready to do whatever it took to bring about the objectives of Jubilee 2000.

What a back!

For me it was also the beginning of the end of my official involvement. My interpretation of the vision that had been given to me was that I was to help start things moving; not necessarily see them through once others with more expertise could take things forward. That I fully intended to honour!

The day continued with me in a happy daze. The sun poured down on us the entire day from a clear blue sky. Everywhere the streets were filled with an amazing bunch of people – babes in buggies, people in wheelchairs, teenagers in outrageous combinations of red items, ordinary churchgoers caught up in something really big, many for the first time in their lives; "I've never done anything like this before" was a common refrain. There were some good talks and discussions in various venues. It was ideal weather for picnics too, outside in the gardens of St Philip's Cathedral.

News quickly spread via the special radio channel FM 105.4, tuned into the walk HQ, that the specific focus of the day – to surround the G8 leaders with a human chain – had gone! The potential numbers who had responded to the invitation to join the chain had caused great alarm among both security forces and those in charge of the G8 meetings (though it was very hard to be too definitive before the event). Indeed, there was such concern over security that the G8 leaders were quickly dispatched at the last minute to a new venue in Weston Park, Shropshire to continue their meetings there.

Human Chain, Birmingham

Initially we were dismayed but it was too late to change the planned day's events. So undaunted, it was agreed that we would continue as planned, making the symbolic chain around Birmingham as a clear signal of the chains of debt that we longed to see broken.

Making the chain

Well before 3 o'clock we all dutifully began moving towards our assigned streets, meeting up again with friends and getting into position. Our South Cave contingent were allocated a section near Queensway. As the church bells began to ring out 3 o'clock we all held hands.

It was an extraordinary feeling with plenty of 'tingle factor' - knowing that all around the city over 70,000 other people were joining hands to make up this human chain. We knew that it was being filmed from the air. I found out later that in some areas the chain was several people deep, but we had to stretch sometimes to reach the next person in our area. Each person mattered. Once we'd formed the chain we chanted, "No more debt, no more debt," blew our whistles with vigour and sang. Nobody really wanted to let go after the assigned two minutes and so we continued. After about 20 minutes we reluctantly broke up our section of the chain. But everywhere the atmosphere was now electric. There was such a sense of achievement.

My designer friend Bill Phelps had cycled down from Leeds on his rickshaw (a long story) and he and a group of friends were enjoying cycling round and round the inner ring road joined by lots of other cyclists. Motorbikes and some initially baffled drivers joined in the party, tooting their horns and waving at a very responsive crowd. A large Japanese contingent from the G8 talks were observed driving around and waving enthusiastically. Taxi drivers were happy to join the party.

Many of the Birmingham regulars and shopkeepers, who had been somewhat wary and even irritated in the morning, were now joining in the party and celebrations, loving the happy, sociable atmosphere. What an amazing day!

In reflection, the human chain proved to be a highly significant event – for a whole variety of reasons. For many of the participants it was their first experience of people power and advocacy at work. With the formation of the coalition a few months earlier, the planning for the day had shown how numerous agencies working together in a generally well-coordinated way could make for a much greater impact.

Rickshaw to Birmingham

The decision of the security forces for the G8 leaders to flee to Weston Park fell rather flat as information reached the delegates both of the scale of the demonstration and of its good nature. Indeed, various delegates and negotiators returned informally to Birmingham to see for themselves what was happening, drawn by the news coverage. And far from being a failure, Tony Blair and other leaders from the G8 summit arranged last minute high profile meetings with Ann Pettifor, Michael Taylor, Bono and other coalition members. Ann commented, "The prime minister has seen the people and he has summoned us to meet him at 5.30 today. In other words, the G8 have backed down. In the face of this people power they've said, 'Wow, we're going to have to listen to this crowd,' so that's very exciting!"

Days after the event, the PM stood up in the House of Commons to "pay tribute to Jubilee 2000 for its dignified and powerful breaking-the-chains demonstration". There was massive coverage by the media and by *The Guardian* in particular, which had dedicated a week to give full coverage of the build-up and the event itself (printing a whole supplement focusing on Jubilee 2000 and the Birmingham event} and continued to give us media coverage following the event.

For the newly formed Jubilee 2000 coalition, it proved a game-changer. Through their campaigning they had forced debt onto the agenda of the G8, albeit with only a small time allocation planned, but through the impact of the Birmingham Chain, debt cancellation was given a much bigger focus during the summit, ultimately leading to a statement on debt on the final day pledging to extend debt relief to more countries (though still within the HIPC initiative). The news coverage obviously played a significant role with plenty of photogenic photos of 'the chain' capturing the imagination. The profile of the Jubilee 2000 coalition was given an enormous boost and the coalition was able to move forward and grow, establishing a larger and very efficient office base with staff building effective political links and establishing networks with many other agencies.

Other groups and campaigns around the world also gained huge encouragement, just as a number of smaller national campaigns were taking off in Peru, Bolivia, Argentina, Guyana, Honduras and Ghana.

For me it had been a taste of heaven – or at least how I rather hope heaven will work out – a party made up of reunions with old friends, meeting interesting and unexpected new friends, united in a common cause, full of surprises and fun, streets free of traffic, people free to wander everywhere and bathed in warm sunshine. It brought a sense of closure to my own involvement in the adventure of the past few years but also a huge sense of anticipation of all that was to unfold.

CHAPTER TWO

The Beginnings

Wednesday, 21st September 1994 was the one day I had really dreaded during a two-week consultancy visit I was carrying out for RURCON and Tearfund, visiting agricultural development projects in Ethiopia, Uganda and Nigeria. Lack of forward planning meant that instead of a direct flight from Addis to Lagos with Ethiopian Airlines, instead we had a 14-hour flight leaving Kampala, Uganda in the early hours to fly to Lagos, including two changes of plane in Nairobi and Doula, with Cameroon Airlines – not, I confess, an airline to inspire great confidence (it ceased trading in 2008). I had particularly asked people to pray for safety in travel on this day. But in addition to answered prayer for safety during the journey, this inauspicious flight was to lead to the unfolding of part of God's plan.

Their planes flew much lower than the more typical 30,000+ feet so we had a wonderful overview of the countries below. Bumpy landings were interspersed with cling-wrapped white cheese sandwiches at two-hourly intervals.

We left green and fertile Uganda in the early morning; Kenya was dry and brown – the short rains having brought little relief that year. We flew over Tanzania and touched down at Bujumbura in Burundi. I studied the faces of the airport staff, wondering about the ethnic mixes and whether Burundi would escape the horrific ethnic violence that had brought such appalling tragedy to neighbouring Rwanda earlier that year. We left the airport, surely one of the most attractive in Africa with its series of cleverly designed tukel-like buildings. As we crossed into what was then Zaire (the Democratic Republic of Congo since 1997), the landscape changed dramatically; firstly, grassy slopes dotted with trees – reminiscent of English parkland – turning later to dense tropical rainforests.

The plane flew low enough during the day to make out all the features in the landscape below and it felt as if the whole panorama of Africa was being unfolded beneath us. Then, it was as if I sensed the voice of God saying to me, "Look at all of this diversity: diversity of landscape, climate, people groups, their leaders and their common striving for economic development. Yet there is one thing linking every country and every person you pass over today. One thing they all have in common. One thing that is pulling the whole of Africa downwards, dragging like a ball and chain as countries limp towards economic development. This is the scandal of Third World debt. No-one and nowhere in Africa escapes its effects." The sense of God's anger at this huge injustice was so vivid and strong, it remained with me through the journey. As I sensed God's anger at this injustice, I was also given his solution: the situation must come to an end. We should not enter the new millennium with this burden in place. The year 2000 was to be a year of Jubilee, when the burdens of Third World debt were cancelled. What an amazing gesture with which to enter the new millennium! What an incredible vision! It lifted my spirits and thrilled me beyond measure. I looked forward to joining in the party!

People would often ask me to explain more about this vision. It wasn't a fleeting 'word of knowledge'; it was rather a gradual emerging and sense of God's concerns that took place over a matter of some time as I gazed out of the windows with time to reflect. Trains and planes can give a sense of being cushioned, of time out of everyday pressures and normality. This day, which I had dreaded, had instead become a prophetic one.

We passed into the thick rainclouds hanging over the fertile plantations of Cameroon and changed planes in the dispiriting airport of Doula before arriving at our destination, Lagos, late in the evening to begin the final stage of the consultancy visit.

The next few days were busy. And on arriving back home in the UK, life was even busier; reports to write, ongoing work, family life to catch up with again, not to mention reading for the Ph.D. I was just beginning. In the cold light of day, the vision I had been given seemed so huge, so unlikely, indeed so ridiculous given the present economic policies of the International Monetary Fund (IMF) and World Bank (WB), I was somewhat embarrassed by it all. I didn't even share it with my husband.

But the vision did not dissipate as I tried to put it behind me. Instead there came the strong feeling that God had given me this vision for a purpose – and that I should take action. It seemed laughable – what could I possibly do? I had no influence, little understanding of the massive economic and political issues involved around international debt, and no time – with ongoing work for Tearfund, a new Ph.D. to get my head round, not to mention three growing youngsters. How on earth could I do anything? And how could I get away from this ridiculous idea that kept nagging at me?

Background to the build-up of the debt crisis

In the 1970s large deposits, mainly from oil wealth, were deposited with Western banks – and they needed to re-lend the money as quickly as possible. Commercial banks and governments in rich countries began lending huge sums to Third World countries. Few questions were asked about the ability of countries to repay these loans. The risks didn't matter too much because governments cannot go bankrupt...?! Leaders interested in taking out loans were not too difficult to find: dictators requiring more supplies of armaments; grandiose building projects; dams, government buildings or irrigation projects. There was no shortage of ways to spend the money. However, there was a great shortage of good advice and careful planning.

Many of the leaders who took out the original loans moved on – out of power. Many of the developments proved of little benefit. Interest rates soared in the 1980s. Countries had already paid back more than they had borrowed and yet were deeper in debt. Several countries declared they simply could not pay their debts and were trapped in a cycle of ever-increasing debt. Desperate to prevent a collapse in the world banking system, the International Monetary Fund (IMF) and the World Bank stepped in to help countries survive. They restructured the loans so that countries could continue to pay the interest but only if they agreed to adopt harsh economic programmes. Such measures included devaluation, diverting resources from basic services such as health and education, privatisation of public services and increasing exports to earn more foreign exchange.

The burden of repaying the debts fell on the poorest in society, people who had rarely seen any benefits from the loans in the first place. By 1996:

- Africa spent four times more on repaying loans than on health care.

- Debtor countries were 60% more in debt than in 1986, simply because of interest rate rises.

- For every £1 given in aid, £3 was taken back in debt repayments.

Despite a variety of economic plans being implemented (notably structural adjustment), sadly, few real benefits resulted. Indeed, the IMF and World Bank sometimes used the opportunity to intervene in debtors' economies. Rising interest rates continued to ensure the debts keep rising. As Susan George noted in her renowned book *The Debt Boomerang,* published in 1992:

It is a triumph of modern statecraft and of international economic management, that neither borrowers nor lenders need play by the rules. It is a triumph of the media's capacity to miss the really big stories, that so few people are aware of it.

No crimes have been committed. The question of justice is another matter entirely!

Chapter Three

Testing the Vision

The first fleece

Two months later a second trip loomed – this time to the United States and Peru; countries I had not visited before. Tiring of the nagging sense that God wanted me to take action on the 'vision' I had been given, I decided that the best way forward was to test the vision with the biblical principal of 'laying down a fleece' – asking for an unlikely response to occur that would help to confirm whether something was indeed of the Lord.[2] So I made a prayerful bargain with the Lord. "OK, Lord," I prayed, "I will share the vision on this trip. If people respond and say they will take action, then I too will take action on my return."

The first few days were at an agricultural workshop with ECHO, a Christian organisation based in Florida. There were nearly a hundred participants, with warm fellowship, teaching and sharing new agri-cultural ideas from around the world. Two sessions were set aside for the informal sharing of new ideas. It would have been so easy to talk about my work with *Footsteps,* the development newspaper that I edited for Tearfund and indeed my reason for attending the workshop. But instead, with much trepidation and some apology, I shared the vision of Jubilee 2000. Afterwards several Americans came up and said dismissively, "It would never work – it would challenge the whole economic order!" A few others were mildly interested in the concept. But then a participant from Tanzania came up to me with tears in his eyes. He shook my hand warmly; "At last someone understands the extent of our suffering from

---

[2] This principle comes from the story of Joshua in Judges 6.

Third World debt. At last, here is an idea that could make a huge difference." He was a student in the United States and said that he would contact a number of his friends and colleagues around the world through the Internet and share the idea.

Here was my response. But it wasn't the only one. Later in Peru, in mid-November I travelled to Taropota with another Tearfund colleague, a Peruvian economist (assessing the impact of a funding grant) and a Tearfund partner, Dr Apolos Landa. I remember the day, a very long one, as one of sweltering heat and atrocious roads. Our destination was a meeting of over eighty pastors in a Bible college in Taropota, where we listened to Apolos deliver a clear and impassioned talk on HIV and lead a lively discussion afterwards. On the long journey home, we stopped for refreshments – fresh coconut juice in shells – and the conversation moved on to other topics. It was a good time to share the vision of Jubilee 2000. All three men seemed amazingly excited by the idea. My Tearfund colleague was full of practical ideas, contacts and suggestions, and offered his London church as a free venue for workshops or meetings. The Peruvian economist took the idea very seriously indeed and later sent me papers from a group of Christian economists in Peru. Apolos was a charismatic Peruvian Church leader and doctor. His response was immediate: "If the West really rises and responds to this idea, then we in the South must also rise to the challenge. If the West will remove the unfair burden of Third World debt, we should rise to meet this by removing the scandal of corruption which affects all levels of government in our country."

Well – I had the answers to my 'fleece' and now had to respond, and actually do something on my return to the UK. But what, and how to begin? I pondered this over Christmas and New Year and at least shared the vision with my husband. No doubt inwardly he sighed and thought, "Yet another crazy idea…" But outwardly he too took it seriously and was supportive, if baffled.

I began ringing around the bigger aid agencies in January – such as Oxfam, CAFOD, Christian Aid and Tearfund – to ask if they would be interested in working on a new initiative regarding Third World debt. They were mildly interested but sceptical. The sense was that if the idea developed then they might consider coming on board a year or two later, but for the present they all had current action plans for their supporters.

Third World debt was something they had all covered to some extent and there was a general feeling that they had 'done debt'. In addition, it was a complex and somewhat boring issue to convey to supporters. I remember George Gelber of CAFOD was particularly helpful in outlining who was doing what and introducing me to the workings of the Debt Crisis Network.

Various conversations simply confirmed my own sense of inadequacy. I lacked the economic and political knowledge to proceed with this on my own. And it was quickly apparent that if no agency was interested in taking the idea further, money, quite a lot of money, would be needed to take things forward. These were two major obstacles that I specifically brought in prayer before the Lord, needing guidance and further confirmation.

Two further fleeces

I prayed that if this vision was to move forward, God would somehow bring to me someone with real expertise and understanding of Third World debt and some funding to take some initial action.

I persisted in my conversations with people from different agencies whenever I had a little time free. Indeed, one conversation would often lead to another, as people would suggest a useful person to contact – which also had the benefit of bringing the call to an end from their perspective! Tearfund had recently produced an excellent and readable report on Third World debt but had not yet raised the subject with their supporters, so there was some definite interest there.

I followed up Gelber's contacts and got in touch with the Debt Crisis Network – a grouping of about forty NGOs who jointly supported a lobbyist (Ann Pettifor) and part time administrator (Angela Wood) to coordinate their action on Third World debt. The Debt Crisis Network had begun in 1987 with the aim of enabling agencies to share in-depth learning and produced regular press cuttings and informative briefings. It was from talking with Angela of the Debt Crisis Network that I first heard of the group Jubilee 2000. I was intrigued – this was just the name I had been given – maybe I need take no further action. What a relief that would be!

Through letters and telephone calls I got to know Martin Dent, an emeritus lecturer in Politics at Keele University, and Bill Peters, a former British ambassador in Uruguay and High Commissioner in Malawi. Both were now retired and dedicating virtually all of their energies to this campaign that they had begun working on together a few years earlier. They were keen to take their ideas forward. Between them they had produced several papers (5,000 to 10,000 words in length) and had circulated these to interested parties. Both immediately sent me copies and welcomed my interest. I sensed that while they had some political and economic leverage, they lacked the experience of producing resources with a wide public appeal, which would have to play a vital part in spreading the idea and in bringing pressure to bear on decision-makers. But in getting to know them, certainly my second fleece was answered. They definitely brought with them the considerable experience and understanding of economics and Third World debt which I lacked.

Bill suggested an initial meeting with them both in London with Ann Pettifor, lobbyist for the Debt Crisis Network and Effie Jordan of World Development Movement. I suggested Tim Chester of Tearfund (author of the recently written Tearfund report on Third World debt) join us. The six of us met for the first time in April 1995 in a basement room that Christian Aid let us use free of charge. It was an informal time, half of which was spent outlining the various positions from which people were coming. Some tentative suggestions were made, including that of employing a campaign strategist to help us plan through a campaign. Ann was positive but wary. I said I would follow things up with her with a further meeting.

That same week I shared the outline of what had been going on at the next meeting of our local World Development Movement group. Debt had always been one of our concerns. I outlined our hopes and the need to find some start-up funding to begin developing resources. After the meeting some dear friends, never ones to make a fuss about things, offered £10,000 – part of a recent family bequest they had received. They said they could think of no better use for it than to launch such a campaign. *Wow!* Just like that – an answer to my third fleece. We had enough funds to make a worthwhile start at least.

A few weeks later, whilst I was en route for meetings at Tearfund, Ann Pettifor made some time for me in her busy schedule – with some reluctance, I sensed. At our first meeting I had explained about how I had felt called to become involved through a vision and was searching to find how best to take things forward. In her own words Ann wrote:

> *I groaned inside and thought – do I need this? But I tried not to show my scepticism too much. I explained how for several years Martin Dent and his friend Bill Peters had been trying to persuade others in the Debt Crisis Network and elsewhere of the value of their idea but to little avail. I explained that we would need money; an office, resources, and the Debt Crisis Network would have to be persuaded to release me to work on the campaign. She left, and I got on with other things. A few months went by and she returned and had made considerable progress. I began to take Isabel Carter very seriously.*

Key personalities

Martin Dent (1924-2014)

Martin was a lecturer in politics at Keele University. He was the archetypal absent-minded academic. Peering through his clouded glasses, with complete indifference to his somewhat dishevelled clothing and appearance, he was never seen without his battered leather briefcase, bursting at the seams with the latest, well-thumbed World Bank tables. Always affable, genuinely interested in everyone he met, he was passionate, focused and knowledgeable about the injustice of Third World debt. As a young man he had worked with the colonial service in Nigeria and was given the position of honorary Chief for the Tiv peoples in Benue state, eastern Nigeria, in honour of his peacemaking efforts there. He was the great-great-great-grandson of Thomas Buxton, the anti-slavery campaigner. When in the late 1980s someone suggested to him that he should take up this campaign against the injustice of international debt, he was quick to make the links with the slavery of Third World debt. In 1990 he launched Jubilee 2000 at Keele University with 2000 signatures. In 2000 he received an OBE for services to international development and debt relief.

Bill Peters (1923-2014)

On leaving Oxford University, Bill Peters worked with the diplomatic service in Ghana (where he helped inspire the young Kofi Annan – then just a schoolboy) and other countries. He then became British ambassador in Uruguay (1977-80) and British High Commissioner in Malawi (1980-1983). He was also a Vice Chair of USPG. Bill was introduced to Martin in 1992, meeting up in a pub in Oxford. They agreed to join forces and work together on Third World debt in 1993. Bill had considerable and influential contacts from around the world, which he used to promote his desire to see debt cancellation. He was focused, careful and a prodigious letter writer.

Together Bill and Martin had approached Gro Harlem Brundtland, at the time chair of the UN World Commission for Environment and Development (former Norwegian Prime Minister), requesting that Norway request the UN to make the year 2000 a 'Jubilee Year'.

Ann Pettifor

Ann was born in South Africa in 1947 with an Afrikaner father and a mother of English descent. She grew up asking awkward questions about apartheid. During university years studying politics and economics in Johannesburg, she grew disillusioned with the Church, though never quite lost her early faith. She developed strong anti-apartheid views, which led to her eventually leaving South Africa for the UK in the late 1960s. Her love of Africa and concern for issues impacting on its people made her a natural choice to run the Debt Crisis Network in 1994, bringing together her experiences of African and Western economies. She brought passion, warmth, clarity of economic and political understanding, particularly over debt, and the ability to think strategically in leading Jubilee 2000.

A final fleece

Martin, Bill, Ann and I agreed to try and form a steering committee and draw together other interested parties. Our first meetings were always informal, and people were free to invite others. Many of my numerous letters at this time were inviting people to join us, and some did, with various comings and goings. Dorothy Logie's name cropped up a number of times, though she only attended once; a Scottish GP very active in campaigning on TWD, she was extremely supportive. Two colleagues from Tearfund became involved; Brendan Bowles (Youth and Student Coordinator) and Tim Chester (Information Officer). Christian Aid were very good to us; Tim Mould, their Director of Regions and Paul Spray, their Head of Policy sometimes attended, and they always provided us with a free meeting room – down in their basement area. Our sociable lunches were held in their large and relaxed staff canteen with its diverse and delicious blend of world foods. Martin was always in his element at lunchtime with a plate of good food in front of him, spluttering crumbs, waving his fork for emphasis and enthusing on a variety of topics close to his heart.

Other members included Tim Greene and Mike Carter (my husband), who were both keen members of our World Development Group; Cathy Brereton was invited by Bill as a key contact from USPG; and Ray Hall came occasionally as a Christian thinker with a particular interest in the millennium.

What were we setting in motion? Our loosely defined aims seemed rather far-fetched and we were an odd group of disparate characters with no organisational base or office. Was this ever going to work? Alarmed by what was now developing, I sought final reassurance from God. Was this the way forward – could our small bunch of 'nobodies' develop a campaign that would honour the vision of Jubilee and debt relief that I had been given? I was full of doubts and questions – and doubly aware that it had been my confidence in the vision that had brought our informal grouping thus far. I prayerfully laid a final fleece.

This was the time of the Toronto blessing; a surprising outpouring of revival and the Holy Spirit which often led to laughing, shaking and ecstatic experiences of God. We had heard a lot about it in our church in North Humberside and were somewhat baffled by it all. Then there was an opportunity to go to a meeting in York, led by a church leader recently returned from Toronto, and maybe experience something of it for ourselves. A group of about thirty of us went along one Saturday. I felt this was a perfect opportunity to ask for God's confirmation on the way forward. I simply prayed that in some way God would use this meeting and time of ministry to speak to me in a personal way and confirm his hand and guidance.

A time of teaching was followed by prayer for the 'blessing' to fall on people. And indeed, all around me were people laughing, falling, shaking and praising God. None of that happened to me. Instead my outstretched hands became heavy – heavier and heavier until they were really painful and hurting. At the same time, I was overwhelmed with sadness and cried and cried. I sensed God saying to me that the burden of Third World debt was overwhelmingly heavy, and I needed to feel his sadness and respond. These physical sensations were things I had never experienced before and made a powerful impact. I took this very personal experience as the direct guidance I was seeking. The vision had not just been a great idea. God's personal calling on me to respond was still there.

In the months and years ahead with the campaign, there were many times of frustration, bafflement and despair. But from that time on, I never doubted the vision. It had been real and was of God, and though I was totally unable to understand why it had been given to me at that time, I never lost sight of it and the sense that all we were doing was pleasing to God.

JUBILEE 2000
and
Lessons of the
World Debt Tables
(1992-93 and 1993-94)

M J Dent
Co-Chair 'Jubilee 2000',
Fellow of Keele University

One of Martin Dent's early booklets

CHAPTER FOUR

Developing Our Communications Strategy

Ann, Martin, Bill and I had very different backgrounds and understanding regarding the debt crisis, but we were clear and united on the solution: linking the year 2000 to the biblical Jubilee concept and using the new millennium as an opportunity to cancel the backlog of unpayable debt. This aim of cancelling the backlog of debt was key; we were not asking for ongoing debt forgiveness, with all the baggage of rights and wrongs implied by this. A one-off cancellation acknowledged that there had been wrongs on the part of both lender and borrower – and removing the backlog of debt (often, in effect, written off by lenders as unpayable anyway) provided a chance to start afresh, without jeopardising the normal sound economic principle of lending money.

The year of the Jubilee is an ancient Hebrew custom recorded in the Bible in Leviticus 25:10, where every 50 years slaves were freed and debts forgiven. We wanted to see the year 2000 claimed as a year of Jubilee when the backlog of unpayable debts would be cancelled for all low-income countries. We wanted freedom for the millions held in the slavery of Third World debt.

My Tearfund colleague from the Peru visit, Dr David Evans, continued to follow up how things were going. During a routine work visit to Tearfund, David met with me, full of news of a contact he had recently made. This person had a decade of experience in advertising and was keen to keep these skills fresh now he had a different career, by helping organisations develop their communications strategies. David was sure he would be a huge help, and so when the issue of how we should communicate with supporters arose at a Jubilee 2000 planning

33

meeting in Christian Aid next day, I suggested his name. This recommendation was one of the innumerable 'God-incidences' that were to become such a feature of the year to follow.

After an introductory letter, I had the first of many phone calls in April 1995 with Mark Greene, then working at London Bible College but keen to continue using his ten years of experience in advertising and the media for freelance work (he is now Executive Director of the London Institute for Contemporary Christianity). His calls were always to the point, often very amusing. He was openly sceptical about the whole idea of Jubilee but intrigued too about our assorted grouping and ridiculously high-flying aims.

In a series of calls, Mark outlined his strategy and charges. His charges were pretty high for our very limited budget (which was still just the £10,000 we had been gifted), though he always seemed to charge us the lowest of any possible rate mentioned. Employing him was a very considerable risk for us given our lack of funds, but given how little time we had to get the 'show on the road', it seemed to make sense. In retrospect it was a hugely important step which helped us clarify what was really important right from the start. He also 'gave us' ideas for many of the effective posters, cartoons and resources that followed.

Once agreement to move forwards was reached, we agreed a meeting date and Mark sent round a lengthy postal survey to all members of the steering group. It contained numerous penetrating questions including:

- What are the major objectives of Jubilee 2000 as you see them?
- What in your view are the core values or biblical principles that underpin the project?
- What excites you about the project?
- How do you think the primary audience feels now about Third World debt?

The questions were circulated, compiled and passed back to Mark before the agreed meeting date of May 26th. On the day, ten of the twelve who had responded were able to attend – Martin; Bill; Ann; Brendan Bowles and Tim Chester, both colleagues from Tearfund; Cathy Brereton of USPG; Ray Hall, architect and author with a particular interest in the millennium; Paul Spray, head of policy at Christian Aid; and Mike

Carter. I note the names simply because this was such an inspirational meeting. I prepared for the meeting with a considerable amount of misgiving, apprehensive of this hard-headed marketing consultant tearing up our precious dreams.

Ann had booked a large room with an overhead projector and Mark brought along a tape recorder. Slight and very intense in manner, he immediately held all our attention. He had compiled a comprehensive strategy document, which he took us through. He aimed to help us draw up a communications strategy, to agree a creative plan – and to consider changing the name. He brought a blast of fresh air and reality into our hardworking but often muddled planning!

He first encouraged participants to share their own perspectives on the significance of Third World debt. Ann, in particular, shared some fascinating insights about Rwanda and Yugoslavia and the impact of Third World debt on what had happened. Martin and Bill revealed the extent of their global contacts and influence, pulling out examples of letters from people in the United Nations, politicians and theologians.

I was really surprised, given his earlier initial scepticism, at Mark's enthusiasm for the campaign. With all his years in the hard-headed business of advertising, he nevertheless believed, having pored over our returned surveys, that our idea had potential. As he went through possible scenarios, his belief that we had a small chance at least was hugely encouraging. Not only that, but ideas for future posters, slogans and cartoons just poured out of him.

- "Give and take; that's what this is all about."
- "Nothing kills faster."
- "Nothing is being done."
- "The quickest way to get money in the hands of the poor is not to take it out."
- "Write off – write now."

I collected them all for future reference. Many became the basis of cartoons in our resources and publicity.

Mark told us that we should fine-tune the overall objective into just one line and suggested this might be "to remove the backlog of unpayable debt from the poor by the year 2000" as this clearly summed up our aim.

We needed to define our ultimate audience – in our case politicians and policy makers – but consider how to use other audiences to reach them. He encouraged us to seek out big, memorable ideas that would be media-friendly and have long-term impact. He noted that it would be a huge problem to capture the public imagination – given that the issue of Third World debt was intrinsically boring and complicated! But he also told us that the media would start looking back 100 or 1000 years and look forward too as the millennium approached. They would be looking for 'big visions'. One of our real assets was that we were offering a radical simple solution instead of complicated half measures.

First priorities

Among our first priorities should be to agree our core message, develop a communications plan, choose a name and logo, decide on high-level patrons and secure funding. And, once we had agreed our core aims and objectives, we should not be tempted to add in additional messages – but to stick with it. From these clear objectives, we could develop resources and publications that would be well informed, positive and with edge!

He was keen for us to choose an alternative name that conveyed more clearly what we had in mind. He felt the name Jubilee came with too many other connotations and for many it would just convey the idea of a royal Jubilee party. It "had no spin for the general public" and needed explanation for most Christians. He felt it would prove really unhelpful. At this point, it's fair to say I had a massive problem with this, given that Jubilee 2000 was the name I had so clearly been given in the vision, but Ann was very taken with this idea and I could see Mark's point of view.

The meeting was one that inspired us all, giving us hope that this campaign could indeed succeed. Ideas and enthusiasm continued to pour out of Mark and we all left feeling fired up and encouraged with a lot of issues to think through.

Mark's enthusiasm and clear-headed thinking had provided some flesh for our dreams. However, probably the most valuable thing he did was to believe in the dream. He was genuinely excited and believed this was indeed of God. His enthusiasm and practical attention to detail fired up Ann in particular.

Tim Chester offered to take the ideas and develop a strategy document for us by the next meeting, which he duly did very effectively.

CHAPTER FIVE

Formalising Our Identity

The meeting which followed on the 11th July 1995 proved another very significant one. It was also Martin's 70th birthday with two cakes provided to his great delight! Knowing there were so many issues to work through, I had allocated responsibilities to steering group members in advance, so they could research various items such as potential patrons, media contacts, NGO entry points and forthcoming key political and economic events that could be targeted. I took on responsibility for investigating registration as a charity and artwork for a logo.

Among the items on the agenda were to agree our mission statement and strategy, to choose a new name, to formalise the structure of the steering group (prior to registration), to plan for an office and staff, and to plan publicity and resources. This was a quite ridiculous quantity of major decision-making to try and cram into four hours. Nevertheless, we got through most of it successfully with Tim Chester's effective chairing – though the choice of name and possible logo remained outstanding. These were so key. No one felt we had yet got the 'right' ones. The proposed mission statement and strategy documents were discussed and amended, and it was agreed that final versions would be signed off at the next meeting – more optimism as actually this took months longer! Plans were made for an introductory public leaflet (which Mark was keen to design for us), a resource pack and an official launch.

Despite the summer holidays (which included an information-gathering trip for me to Uganda to begin preparations for my doctoral research), everyone continued to beaver away on their respective priorities. There was encouraging news too that at last the World Bank had acknowledged that there was a problem with multilateral debt and that action was needed (news that had horrified the IMF).

Decision time for the name and strapline

The agenda for the September 18th meeting was again ridiculously ambitious. We simply had to decide on name, logo, patrons, launch, employees, office, funding, content of resource pack and leaflet; not to mention keeping up-to-date with all the happenings regarding Third World debt. By now several new people had joined our steering group, including Will Reid, a retired banker with a keen interest in global economics. Again, we only had four hours for our deliberations. Mark came back again for this meeting, partly out of interest and partly to help finalise plans for the leaflet which he had been working on for us.

It's worth mentioning that we would often pause at some point during these meetings – as we discussed weighty matters – and gulp or laugh at how our small group was making such huge plans to 'change the world' – or at least the world of debt rescheduling and repayments and those who suffered from its consequences. Who on earth did we think we were, we would muse? Where were the people of consequence and influence (and well-funded campaigns) who should be with us? But the moment would pass, and we would return to the issue under question. Certainly, Christian Aid's basement rooms, where we invariably met, were put to very good use indeed by 'a bunch of nobodies'.

Some of the suggested name options

Fresh Start	Quits 2000	Eat the Elephant
Release 2000	Debtfree 2000	Clean slate 2000
Tide 2000 (turning the tide)	Jubilee 2000	The Big Wipeout
	Renew 2000	DropDebt 2000
Stamp out Debt		

This was crunch time for the name. Numerous options had been bandied about in the previous few months. However, these were now refined down to the top two contenders – Debtfree 2000 and Jubilee 2000. Tensions ran high and there was much debate, but in the end, we agreed it would be decided by an open and democratic vote, during which I, for one, held my breath. To my great surprise, both Mark and Ann changed their minds at the last moment. And so 'Jubilee 2000' it was by 5 votes to 3 with 2 abstentions. For me personally, though I could see the value and clarity of Debtfree 2000, it had none of the resonance of Jubilee – and of course this was so clearly the name I had been given in the vision. It was also the name that Martin and Bill had been using for several years. Mark noted that because Jubilee was a Hebrew name, it was the same word in nearly all European languages. After the lengthy discussions regarding the name, the strapline was agreed immediately and unanimously as "a debtfree start for a billion people".

The final version of the strategy document, on which Tim Chester had invested a lot of time, was agreed with a few additions and amendments. Now at last we had an official document that could be submitted to potential funders and patrons. And after several months of uncertainty, we could now develop some temporary letterheaded paper, which would be helpful in approaching funders whilst we agreed on an official logo.

Following an initial bid to the Lotteries Charities Fund, I agreed to submit further requests for staff, office and campaign costs to the Rowntree's Trust and the Cooperative Bank.

The 'No owe' logo

I had commissioned several possible ideas for logos from two freelance artists – unsure at the time of which name would be selected. None of their ideas had met with very much enthusiasm from steering group members but at least enabled us to have something temporary to use for letterheaded paper and funding applications in the meantime. The search would continue.

Several months later, I passed around initial ideas for a logo which had been designed for us free of charge by Bill Phelps, a designer and good friend of mine from Wingfinger Graphics and his brother-in-law Brendan (of Tearfund). They represented the digits for the number 2000 as a chain, with a break in the central loop. In addition, they had arranged the digits so that they could also be read as "No O" – i.e. "No owe". They told us that they had simply played around with the name over a coffee break.

Developing the logo –

Reminiscences from Brendan Bowles and Bill Phelps

During the lengthy deliberations over the name of the campaign, Isabel asked two artists to develop some ideas for a logo, assuming that the most likely name would be 'Stamp out Debt 2000' or 'Debt free 2000'. They developed some useful ideas, particular around the idea of 'Stamp out Debt' but had no inspiration at all regarding a logo for the name Jubilee 2000.

Brendan began doodling some ideas and sketches for the logo whilst on the train going to a management meeting at Christian Aid in July 1995. He obviously continued doodling during the meeting (from his scribbled-over meeting notes) and must have showed his ideas to Isabel that day as, with her encouragement, he then forwarded some tidied-up sketches to his brother-in-law Bill Phelps (already very familiar to Isabel as he was doing the design work for her Tearfund work), for him to develop further.

This design was shown to the committee chaired by Brendan on 12/12/95 under 'Any Other Business'. Isabel's minutes for the meeting record, "A logo had been designed by Wingfinger Graphics using the letters 2000 as chains and saying 'No owe'. This met with general approval. A break in the chain was suggested. We would then have a logo which stated our purpose (no owe) used the Jubilee year 2000 (our message), and which showed the chains of debt breaking (our ultimate goal)."

Subsequently, Wingfinger Graphics finalised the design of the well-known logo. The same basic design is still in use today by numerous debt agencies around the world. Brendan comments, "In my view Bill's typography and his polishing of the graphic is absolutely brilliant and a vital component of the impact of the campaign."

Early image and logo ideas

There's an interesting follow-up to the story of the logo. As the millennium was approaching, Adrian Lovett got in touch with Bill and asked if Jubilee 2000 could buy sole rights for the use of the logo. We'd already been paid for our design work, so I signed some heavy-looking legal documents that transferred the copyright for the sum of £1. (I think maybe I inserted a clause that allowed Wingfinger Graphics to use it in its own publicity.)

Bill adds, "I don't think I have any record of Jubilee 2000 ever paying us that £1. But in the spirit of the campaign, we decided to write it off. In full…!"

The Jubilee 2000 logo

The logo served us well for the next four years and saved us a fortune in commissioning one from a designer; another of God's wonderful provisions. And with minor amendments, the logo continues to be used today by the Jubilee Debt Campaign, though the numbers no longer spell out "no owe", a detail that few ever noticed anyway!

Charity and company status

Since none of the larger charities approached had been willing to take us under their wing, in the autumn of 1995 I researched how to obtain both charity status and registration as an incorporated company with a group called the Industrial Common Ownership Movement (ICOM) in Leeds. This small organisation proved wonderfully helpful in steering us through a complicated process. It was not straightforward, taking the best part of a year to obtain, and there was much correspondence regarding the political nature of the campaign.

In February 1996, Bill and Brendan went to a meeting of the Charity Commissioners in London, where the Commissioner explained that we would not qualify for full charity status because of the political nature of our aims. Our charter would need to remove reference to "campaigning". But they conceded that one way around this dilemma would be to split the activities, with a charitable educational side and a campaigning wing; advice much along the lines of that provided by ICOM. So we proceeded with not one but two applications.

The aims for both of these had to be put in writing together with samples of the resource materials we were planning. All these delays meant we were still six to eight weeks away from receiving that all-important charity number for the leaflet, not to mention other resources, as crunch time for publishing approached.

A reminder of the voluntary and somewhat ad hoc way in which we worked comes from a gentle complaint from Helen Barber of ICOM on the 28th March 1996, when Bill Peters had written a long letter somewhat contradicting what had been previously agreed with them regarding pursuing Jubilee 2000 as a charity and company limited by guarantee. He was obviously concerned that I might have missed some of the finer details in my communications with ICOM!

Helen wrote, "Mr Peters has been contacting our office rather a lot of late and in order to avoid confusion and potential problems, we do have a strong policy of only communicating with the named contact, unless instructed otherwise by the organization itself."

INTRODUCING JUBILEE 2000

 Billions of people in the world's poorest countries are enslaved by debt. Debts run up by governments on their behalf. Debts which started as easy credit pushed by rich lenders. Debts which the poor will never be able to repay. Debts which enrich lenders, but leave children malnourished, while families live in desperate poverty.

Jubilee 2000 believes the time has come to do something about it.

Our aim is to celebrate the new millennium by lifting the burden of unpayable debt from the poorest countries. We want to do this by producing a clear, workable **Jubilee Proposal**:

- **a one-off cancellation...**
- **by the year 2000...**
- **of the backlog of unpayable debt...**
- **owed by the world's poorest countries...**
- **on a case by case basis.**

Our aims

Helen Barber of ICOM did a wonderful job of steering us through all the hurdles, and in May we finally got formal approval from the charity commission to set up as an educational charity and a company limited by guarantee. ICOM charged less than £1,000 for their work over the past seven months. Without their guidance it would undoubtedly have taken us a lot longer and might well have proved unsuccessful.

Five members of the steering group agreed to become trustees of the new charity – Martin, Bill, Tim Greene, Will Reid and me. In June 1996 the new trustees filled in the forms to become trustees and directors of the new charity and company. We had to formalise appointments within the charity and company, appointing Chair, Treasurer and Secretary. We had to work out how to split the different aspects of our work to maintain clear channels of work and funding for both charity and company. We also now had to produce official quarterly reports. All pretty challenging for a large organization and certainly so for our small voluntary grouping!

However, following these developments, we rarely had separate meetings – these just continued as before with others attending as available, but with more attention given to keeping an accurate record of meetings. We began to call ourselves the Jubilee 2000 Management Committee rather than just a steering group.

Patrons

Following Mark Green's advice, several members of the committee spent much time approaching numerous high-profile people asking them to consider becoming patrons. We also wrote to several musicians including Bruce Cockburn and Graham Kendrick to see if they might feel inspired to write a song on the topic.

For example, among the first ones to be approached were:

- HM The Queen   Bill to approach through Private Secretary
- President Nelson Mandela   Bill to approach through Washington Okuma
- Cardinal Hume   Ann to approach
- Archbishop George Carey   Isabel to approach through Bishop of Hull

- Sir Edward Heath   Bill to approach
- Jimmy Carter   Brendan to approach
- Baroness Chalker   Bill to approach
- Sir Leon Brittan   Martin to approach
- Paddy Ashdown   Martin to approach
- Tony Blair   Martin to approach
- John Major   Martin to approach
- President Kaunda   Ann to approach
- Richard Branson   Isabel to approach
- Bob Geldof   Isabel to approach

Of those approached, approximately three quarters of people turned it down: "too busy", "need more time to consider the issue" or "I've done my bit". Richard Branson sent a very polite apology, noting he already had too many commitments but wishing us luck. The Rt. Hon. Sir David Steel was apologetic that he would have little time to give us as he was trying to shed responsibilities, but he was very happy to contribute his name to the cause.

And thankfully, others too were happy to give their name to the initiative:

I am very impressed with your Jubilee 2000 campaign and how very well thought out your particular positions are. They are quite persuasive .... and not just vague and dreamy idealism but pragmatic and equitable...

Most Rev. Desmond Tutu

I do wholeheartedly subscribe to the aims and purpose of Jubilee 2000 and am more than happy therefore to lend my name to it.

Rt. Revd James Jones, Bishop of Hull

I should regard it as a great honour to be associated with Jubilee 2000 and anything I can do to give it greater prominence, I would be happy to do.

John Simpson, BBC

I appreciate your realistic and considered approach to progress on this issue.

Glenys Kinnock MEP

Tim Greene and I met with James Jones, the Bishop of Hull in March 1996, shortly after he had agreed to become a patron, since we were both in his Diocese. He was quite inspirational and full of enthusiasm. He was full of ideas on how we might catch the public imagination locally – maybe inviting Nelson Mandela to Hull for the 700th anniversary of Hull City in 1999 (in fact Desmond Tutu was later invited as the guest of honour). He suggested commissioning a roving international ambassador who might arrive by helicopter from Trinity Square, Hull after he had ceremoniously 'washed his hands' of the evil of debt in the font where Wilberforce was baptised. He suggested that he and Desmond Tutu might speak to the Anglican Synod in 1998.

His comments included, "I have never heard of such a huge project," and, "You have to have an extremely capable Coordinator to 'catch the public imagination' and to provide a source of imaginative ideas." In addition, he commented wisely, "Forget the religious press – you have to capture the attention of the national media." His inputs and enthusiasm initiated some notable debt cancellation events in Hull in the following years.

Raising the profile of issues

Bishop James Jones noted that at their Committee meetings a group of environmentalists apparently spend 5 minutes discussing issues and 1 hour 55 minutes discussing stunts to raise the profile of these issues – and suggested this should be a pattern for us to follow in the future. He felt our leaflet was still too detailed and hard to read for busy people but accepted that it would be fine for sympathisers.

When I now look back at the files for this year, I am astonished by the number of letters and responses, written and received from a huge array of people, in between meetings. And in this I know that Martin and Bill excelled and were even more prolific.

Cartoon from the Debt Cutter's Handbook

CHAPTER SIX

Our Launches

Reading back through the minutes, it's amusing to look back over our various plans to launch. We were always too ambitious. On the one hand, it was desperately urgent to get our message out, firstly in order to mobilise potential supporters to take action, and secondly to help raise the funding necessary for us to become a viable entity. On the other hand, if we tried to do this before we could come over as a professional charity, with staff, funding and a functioning office, we could do ourselves huge damage. Without a central office in place to follow up enquiries and without the Jubilee Charter in hand, it could prove a fiasco.

We planned first to launch during the African Leaders Tour – a week of activities planned by the Debt Crisis Network in February 1996 bringing African leaders to Europe. We had permission to launch as the culmination of that week – at an evening event on 10th February. There would be a conference that Saturday with about 400 committed people from a number of NGOs likely to be present, followed by an evening concert with many young people present – many just for the music. We would need to provide a well-known patron to speak in the afternoon and then again for five minutes in the evening, and to provide people to run a stall and cope with the anticipated 'hundreds' of people signing up for membership!

But a month or so earlier, we realised that there was no way we could be ready in time. We contented ourselves with simply publicising Jubilee 2000 using some temporary leaflets that Mike Carter put together, providing resources on Third World debt, and providing a mailing list for interested people to sign up to. However, in the end we were also generously given thirty minutes on the platform at the main highlight event of the week on 10th February when Kenneth Kaunda would be speaking among others, to share information about Jubilee 2000. As a consequence, the mailing list gathered about 200 names and addresses.

At a meeting a few weeks later, Tim Moulds made the helpful comment that launches work really well once groups have been going for at least three years! We planned to *have our aims met* within four years...

Susan George, one of our new patrons and author of the influential book *The Debt Boomerang,* had offered to come and speak at a workshop for us on Saturday, April 13th 1996, around which we could launch ourselves. This was an offer which was much appreciated. However, in view of the fact we were still unlikely to have any employees *in situ* until April/May, the logistics of organising such a conference in the end proved too difficult. We could not run the risk of this being a flop. The decision was made regretfully to write to Susan and ask to arrange a later date (which in the end sadly never happened).

Whilst actual launches were still under discussion, we did manage to launch a first website in January 1997 – at the time more for the benefit of supporters in the USA as so few UK supporters were likely to make use of this, given the lack of Internet access. How times change!

Despite the lack of an official launch, opportunities for sharing information about Jubilee 2000 were never lacking. As word spread through our contacts and initial articles, so opportunities to speak rolled in; sometimes to church groups, world development groups, local Mother's Union groups, university groups – or to preach in church services. All of us on the steering group noted and shared out these opportunities in the early months.

Various national Jubilee 2000 launches took place in the United States (in June 1997), in Germany (in September 1997), Italy (February 1998), Jubilee 2000 Afrika (April 1998), Latin America (January 1999) and Peru (March 1999), and there were many others. However, in the UK it was the launch of the UK Jubilee 2000 Coalition that came nearest to an official launch, in October 1997.

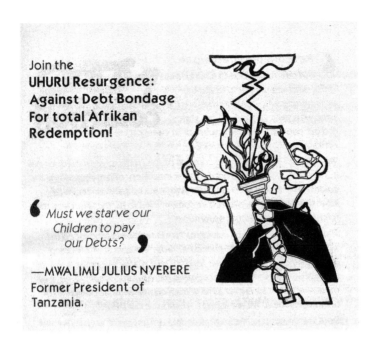

Join the
UHURU Resurgence:
Against Debt Bondage
For total Afrikan
Redemption!

❛ *Must we starve our*
    Children to pay
      our Debts? ❜

—MWALIMU JULIUS NYERERE
Former President of
Tanzania.

Afrika campaign leaflet

CHAPTER SEVEN

The Sauda Leaflet

The Jubilee 2000 leaflet produced in the summer of 1996 was probably the most important document we ever produced in terms of its impact. Mark Greene was really keen to help with it using his experience and design skills, charging far less than his usual rates. We planned a folded A4 sheet with which to catch people's attention, to explain what Jubilee 2000 and Third World debt were about, to inspire people with our solution and then to have an additional fold to encourage them to give us the money we so desperately needed to get things up and running (without damaging the rest of the leaflet). No small challenge then! Those were the days before email distribution lists – and long before Twitter and Facebook took off.

The first efforts were very wordy but slow progress was made in editing down the details without dumbing down the content. Rather than a typical layout, we agreed that the centre spread would show the circle of debt. Key facts were highlighted in text boxes – "The best way to get money into the hands of the poor is to leave it there... Africa now spends four times more on interest on its loans than on health care." Slimming down our message into a few short and pithy paragraphs involved hours of effort. Trying to explain the intricacies and impact of Third World debt in a few sentences was anathema to Bill and Martin – and it helped to have Mark, rather than me, as the person doing most of the editing down. But in the end, they proved understanding and we were all able to sign off the final version in January. We had no funds to do a second leaflet, so we had to get it right first time.

Mark and I agreed that a newborn babe would be ideal for the first page – and also for a poster design – to illustrate just how incredibly unfair Third World debt was in its impact. I rang around some good photographers who worked for development agencies, trying to find someone about to travel to Africa. I had a positive response from Jenny Matthews, who did a lot of work for Oxfam and was about to travel to Rwanda for an assignment. She agreed that she would somehow fit in the time to find and photograph a newborn babe. During her work there, she fitted in a visit to a maternity hospital in Kigali, Rwanda and took various photographs of newborns. As a professional, she needed little briefing in order to be able to explain to the mothers what she was doing and check whether they were willing to have a photo of their baby used for this purpose.

A couple of weeks later she sent through a contact sheet with photos of seven babies in various angles to choose from. I still remember poring over the contact sheet with friends Diana and Kathryn, cup of tea in hand, one afternoon in early November. We settled on the baby daughter of Sauda Mzamu-kunda, born at 3pm on 28th October 1995. Babies are not named until the eighth day in Rwanda, so we had no name to go on and instead simply used the mother's name. It would be very interesting if someone could track her down today... After the genocide of the previous year, it seemed a symbol of hope to be able to choose a Rwandan baby.

Having chosen 'Sauda', the headline message to grab people's attention on both leaflet and accompanying flyer was, "Sauda is one day old. She already owes 30 times more than she will earn in her lifetime." It was a powerful and sobering means of expressing the huge unfairness of Third World debt.

However, before we could print the leaflet, a number of pieces of information had to be included – all of which were essential. We had to wait for the approval (if granted) of the charity commissioners to add in a charity number. Not only would this bring in additional income via gift aid, but it would provide a very necessary reassurance to the general public that we were a genuine and trustworthy setup. We needed a postal address and we needed to agree on the logo and strapline. And if these were not forthcoming in time, we would miss the window of opportunity with the mailings which had been agreed with agencies. There were many fraught days and nights of waiting once the content was agreed.

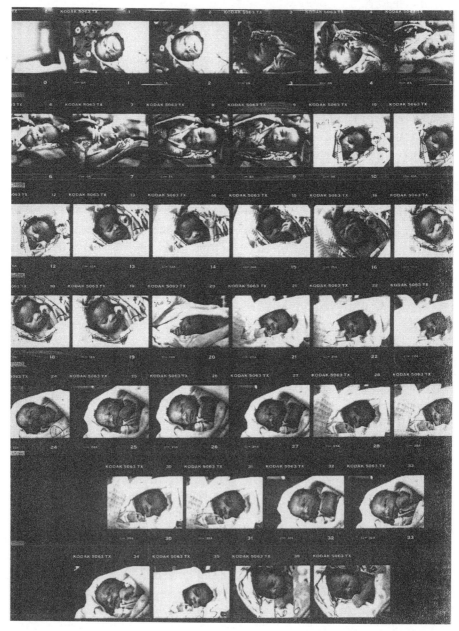

Baby images

We heard back from the charity commissioners in July 1996 with the wonderful news that our application had been successful. This would reassure potential new supporters and meant that we could now claim gift aid on donations and apply for charitable grants.

Sorting out an office address was another a complicated nightmare with all kinds of documents awaiting printing and decisions pending. Even with obtaining the go-ahead to use a small office in Christian Aid, we knew we might need to plan for growth, so we wanted a memorable P.O. Box number that could move with an office move. Cathi Brereton of USPG had applied on our behalf for P.O. Box 2000, which she was told was available. However, when confirmation was finally received, the day before the go-ahead for printing, we had been allocated the memorable P.O. Box 7936. Despite anxious fax and phone calls, there was no give. It was P.O. Box 7936 or a few other equally unmemorable numbers. So at the very last minute I went back to Tim in Christian Aid and asked if there was any way we could use their address (P.O. Box 100). To my great relief they agreed to this, after consultation.

Aware now of just how protective agencies are of 'their supporters', I am amazed by how generous several of the bigger agencies were in distributing our leaflet – which was, after all, unashamedly launching a new organisation and asking for funding to establish this. The leaflet was printed in July 1996. Among those who distributed this for us were USPG (8000 copies), World Vision (85,000 copies) and Tearfund (135,000 copies). Indeed, Tearfund broke all their usual rules regarding distributing other organisations' publicity. They distributed a staggering number for us, inserting them in their quarterly newsletter, all free of change once we had them delivered to their mailing house. The cost to us of this huge print run of 150,000 was £7,500, which was a massive outlay on our exceedingly limited budget. It was a huge step of faith.

The response

The response to the leaflet was extraordinary. It basically provided all the funding that we needed to pay our two new staff over the next few months.

Sauda is one day old

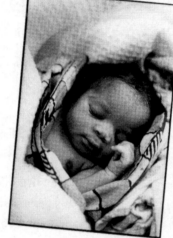

She already owes 30 times more than she will earn in her lifetime

JUBILEE 2000
A debt-free start for a billion people

Sauda leaflet

The deadly spiral of debt

TRAPPED

A billion people are trapped. Trapped in poverty they can do nothing about. Trapped under a mountain of debt they can never pay back.

Africa now spends four times more on interest on its loans than on health care.

MONEY TO LEND

In the 1970s Western banks had a lot of money to lend. They lent huge sums to Third World countries hoping to boost exports and make a profit.

OUT OF CONTROL

Then two things happened which sent the debts of Third World countries spiralling out of control:

- Interest rates rose massively – so debt repayments rocketed.

- The prices of basic commodities

In the world's 37 poorest countries, spending per person has gone down 50% on health and 25% on education.

went down by 30% on average so Third World incomes nose-dived.

Debt fuels the drug trade as poor farmers turn to growing high value cash crops such as opium & cocaine.

In 1982 the World Bank and the International Monetary Fund stepped in. The good news was they gave the debtors more time to pay.

CHAOS

The result was chaos. The poorest countries in the world were suddenly earning less and having to pay back much more.

The rainforests are being destroyed to provide timber and beef to earn foreign currency to pay back debts.

The bad news was that accepting their conditions meant poor governments had even less to spend on their people. And the debts went on rising…

Debt means many countries can't afford imports. This helped cause global recession and a rise in Western unemployment.

DEEP DEBTS

Today many of the world's poorest nations are even deeper in debt. Though they may have repaid the equivalent of the original loan many times over, still their total debts continue to rise.

Over 500,000 children die each year because of cutbacks to health services.

Everyone agrees that parts of the debts can never be repaid. With their own loans, banks have set aside money to cover that possibility. But they haven't cancelled the debts. And while the debts remain Sauda can never be free.

In 1993 rich nations took back £3 in debt repayments for every £1 they gave in aid.

For a billion people development is being thrown into reverse. After decades of steady economic advance, large areas of the world are sliding back into poverty.

There is a solution!

Turn to the back page to find out what it is…

Centre page of the Sauda leaflet

The generosity and response of people was heart-warming. Given that this brief leaflet was all they had to go on to let them know about Jubilee 2000, the issue of Third World debt and our aims to tackle it, it nevertheless touched a chord. Donations of £4,000 and £5,000 were received alongside the more usual £5 or £10 cheques.

The leaflet encouraged people to become members and to set up a direct debit form in return for which they would receive the *Debt Cutter's Handbook*[3] and four newsletters a year. For us this helped provide a regular and growing income. For the donors it automatically ended at the end of 2000 – which must have encouraged many more people to join in since it was not open-ended.

Writing to Roger Northcott of the Tudor Trust in October 1996, I noted that four months after distributing the leaflet, we had received £23,526 in donations from supporters and had over 600 people signed up as members. Memos from Celia, our administrator at the time, describe the volume of letters and cheques received in response to the leaflet: "I'm up to my tonsils," she commented! This generosity meant that although (as usual) we lacked the whole amount, we decided to go ahead and appoint a communications officer to help service this growing membership. Nick Buxton joined the staff in October, as a temporary Communications Officer but later becoming a permanent staff member.

---

[3] See Chapter 9 on page 62.

CHAPTER EIGHT

Agreeing the Charter

The need for a clear and non-negotiable Jubilee charter was referred to at virtually every meeting during 1995. We all knew the importance and great urgency of this – a document that clarified our aims and would withstand scrutiny by both politicians and economists. The charter needed to have an easy-to-understand introductory paragraph or two which could be used in all our publicity, followed by detailed information on exactly what we were proposing, which would provide the basis of economic negotiations. But the detailed and lengthy discussion it required was hard to find during our busy steering group meetings. Many of us, including me, had little to add to the detail, other than being aware that the final outcome needed to be precise, non-negotiable and readable.

The IMF and World Bank as the biggest lenders were not opposed to debt relief but they were well aware of the constraints and counter-arguments; in particular that if all debt was cancelled, it would simply encourage wealthy countries to stop lending and to cut aid budgets still further.

The announcement of the first HIPC agreement in 1996, just as Jubilee 2000 opened our office and 'went public', was a complete coincidence. It was a start but didn't go nearly far enough. We were asking for at least $350bn to be cancelled in order to make a real difference and wanted 52 countries, including another 11 excluded from the current HIPC process, to benefit from urgent debt relief.

We were aware that useful comparisons might be made with the Marshall plan at the end of World War II which used a number of innovative financial interventions to enable Western European countries to rebuild their battered economies. We wanted our charter to be seen as similarly innovative and effective.

A meeting (optimistically called the final meeting to agree the charter – but alas not!) was arranged for 24th January 1996 in Christian Aid at 12pm to try and resolve the charter. Martin, Will Reid and Bill had long been involved in preparing this document and were now busily engaged in gathering information on secondary market prices, calculating the likely costs of debt release – all based on information for 1994 – which would be available in the new World Debt tables about to be released. Will pursued his contacts at the *Financial Times,* if necessary paying for consultants and expertise. Other economists were invited, along with Ann, to benefit from their advice and involvement.

Of course, there was no way this was the final meeting. Nevertheless, it resulted in a draft charter that continued to be deliberated and argued over much of that year (I still have various scribbled over versions). An alternative version was then produced by Ann, removing the arguments and unnecessary details, and focusing purely on our requests. Will then did a wonderful job in trying to combine the two versions into something that all would feel able to sign off.

The draft introduction for the charter was ready for use in the handbook and leaflet as planned. A final third draft, which was a modest three pages in length, was widely distributed for consultation with supporters prior to final endorsement by 31st October 1996.

The Initiative on Heavily Indebted Poor Countries (HIPC) in brief

The HIPC initiative was launched in 1996 by the IMF and World Bank aiming to cut debt repayments to sustainable levels. But it came with various strings attached – in particular, the need for countries to first show a sound economic record for six years. The IMF imposed strict Structural Adjustment Programmes. And it proved very slow – by the beginning of the year 2000 debt relief had only been given to Uganda, Mozambique, Bolivia and Guyana.

The Jubilee 2000 Charter

The Jubilee 2000 Charter suggests a solution to the problem of Third World debt which is attractive to both debtors and creditors. It proposes the remission – by 31 December 2000 – of the unpayable debts owed by highly indebted poor countries to commercial banks, creditor governments and multilateral bodies (such as the International Monetary Fund, the World Bank and Regional Development Banks).

The Jubilee 2000 Charter proposes that:

- **There is an overwhelming need for remission of the backlog of unpayable debts owed by highly indebted poor countries. Debt remission should relate to commercial, government and IMF/World Bank debts, and debt reduction should comprehensively include all three forms of debt.**
- **Creditors as well as debtors must accept responsibility for these high levels of indebtedness.**
- **The remission should be a one-off, unrepeatable act, tied to the celebration of the new millennium. It would set no precedents for future loans.**
- **The precise details of remission should be worked out in consultation with both creditors and debtors for each debtor country.**
- **These details should be agreed by arbitrators nominated in equal numbers by both creditor and debtor, under the aegis of the UN.**
- **Their deliberations should be transparent and well-publicised, taking into account for each debtor country, that country's probity, economic management, social policies and human rights record.**
- **Funds available after the remission of debt should be channelled into policies which benefit the poor, in line with UNICEF's recommendations for investment in social development.**
- **Low income countries – with an annual income per person of less than US $700 – should receive full remission of all unpayable debt.**
- **Higher income countries – with an annual income per person between US $700 and US $2,000 – should receive partial remission.**

The Jubilee 2000 Charter is offered as a model for a workable and acceptable solution to the problem of poor country debt. It would create a new, disciplined beginning to financial relations between North and South, and a fresh start for millions of the world's poor.

The Jubilee 2000 Charter

CHAPTER NINE

The Debt Cutter's Handbook

A freelance editor, Ingrid Hanson, was chosen and began work on the resource pack in November 1995. Details of contents and approach were discussed and considered in order to brief her. We agreed the pack should have three aims: to inform and motivate; to facilitate the sharing of information; and to encourage action. It would act as our main resource to fully equip 'ordinary' people. It had to explain the issues behind the complex debt spiral in a way that led people to initiate action – not just individually but in small groups and churches.

Background information should be combined with case studies, outlines of talks, artwork for overhead projector slides, plenty of ideas for action, sample forms for 'unchain' letters, collecting signatures etc. It should contain a 'dummies' guide to debt tables, cartoons, discussion starters etc. I spent a lot of time gathering materials and articles for Ingrid to work with. For example, our older daughter wrote one of the sample letters included to our MP.

In our typical way of doing things, we employed her knowing that we had enough funding available to pay her as editor, but with nothing available as yet for the design work and printing. We certainly had experience of working in faith! We agreed two parallel packs would be prepared – a general version and a church version – with most pages in common but allowing us to insert additional Bible studies and sermon outlines for Christians on the Jubilee principle.

5 GETTING YOUR HANDS DIRTY

What does the Bible say?
Material for talks and discussions

1 Jubilee Deuteronomy 15:1-15

The principle of Jubilee is central to Old Testament teaching and is designed largely to protect the poor Loans were given to people who had fallen into poverty through sickness, war or any other adversity, including poor judgement. So the Year of Jubilee was a way of ensuring that they were not kept in poverty or slavery forever

The principle of Jubilee is about community – a recognition that the Israelites were accountable to one another They were to lend freely to the poor, without interest. They were not to take away the livelihood of the poor to ensure they would pay their debts (Deuteronomy 24:8). The Jubilee year meant that no-one would be permanently indebted or enslaved, but would have the opportunity to begin anew, and have freedom, land and possessions restored.

In a world where we talk freely of economic communities, the mutual accountability of community has gone out of international economics. Individualism and greed have become commonplace and caring for the poor has become an added act of personal generosity, not a responsibility of the better-off.

International debt is a supreme example of this, where the rich nations perpetuate the slavery of the poor through debt, and in the process feed their own domination and greed. Yet the rich nations share the responsibility for Third World debt with the rulers of the poorer nations. Applying the Jubilee principle to the thorny issue of Third

World debt would lead, as it did for the Israelites, to a new start – not just for the poor, but for the whole international community.

Discussion

How does the principle of Jubilee translate into our personal and business lives? What can we do to ensure that it is put into practice in some way at a national level? How should we as Christians and as nations approach the issue of loans – should we charge interest? Should we only loan to the creditworthy? (see Luke 6:32-35)

Talk it through!

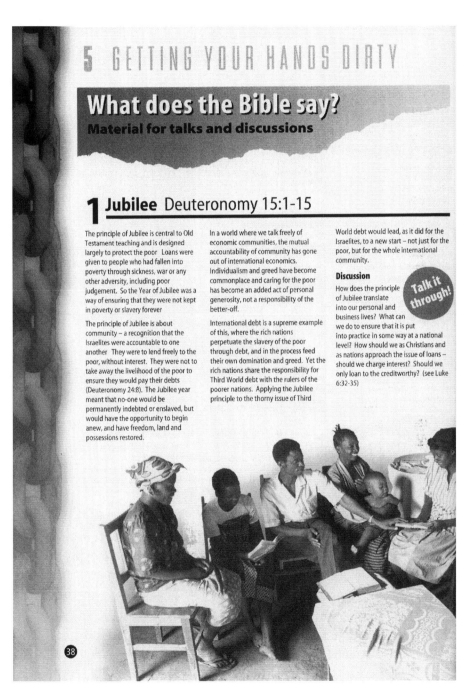

38

Bible study from the Church version of the Debt Cutter's Handbook

Ingrid brought her initial drafts to the meeting in December. She had followed a helpful structure – explaining the problem, possible solutions and then our answer. Initial sample pages came over as too cluttered and busy, with no ideas for discussion and action. The group also felt that our big idea was Jubilee – so the resource pack needed to start with an eye-catching opening, outlining our idea and the concept behind it. This idea should then run through the pack – emphasizing its distinctiveness on each page. The original plan was to have this ready to distribute and sell during Debt Crisis Network's African tour in February 1996 (our original planned launch date), but when our launch was put back, it allowed more time to get the content right.

Several of Mark Greene's throwaway comments were used to produce copyright-free cartoons for use in overhead projectors, posters and newsletters, using a good friend Rod, in Yorkshire, to produce the drawings. I'm amused to be reminded that I even dragged my vicar into researching dates for the fall of Jericho for one cartoon – "And the walls came tumbling down... Jericho 1240BC, Berlin 1989, South Africa 1994, Third World Debt 2000?

Reminiscences from Bill Phelps of Wingfinger Graphics, a colleague and friend via my Tearfund work.

Wingfinger Graphics' first involvement with Jubilee 2000 was in 1995 when we produced some initial leaflets as the organisation was just beginning to coalesce.

In 1996 we started work on the 48-page 'Debt Cutter's Handbook' (a title of our own devising) which was later substantially updated as 'Breaking the Chains'. Both these books were designed to combine the basic facts of international debt with guidelines for effective campaigning on the issue.

'Breaking the Chains' was greatly enhanced by the work of some of the country's leading political cartoonists, including Steve Bell, Chris Riddell and Dave Brown.

I became personally involved in the campaign. Designing and constructing a 7-foot under-arm loan shark and pedalling a cycle rickshaw from Leeds to Birmingham, then Cologne and finally to

Genoa via the Alps are not free services that we offer to all of our clients at Wingfinger Graphics – but we're extremely fortunate to be able to work for people who share our global concerns, and there is a tendency for us to get drawn into their various schemes to end poverty.

Cover of The Debt Cutter's Handbook

The No 1 casualty of Third World debt has almost disappeared...

JUBILEE 2000
A debt-free start for a billion people

Cartoon from the Debt Cutter's Handbook

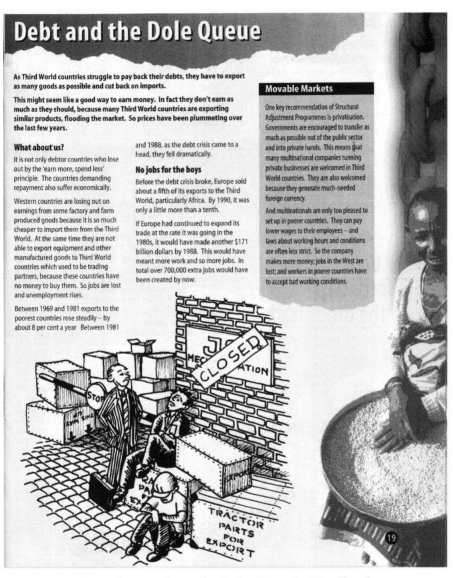

Debt and the Dole Queue

As Third World countries struggle to pay back their debts, they have to export as many goods as possible and cut back on imports.

This might seem like a good way to earn money. In fact they don't earn as much as they should, because many Third World countries are exporting similar products, flooding the market. So prices have been plummeting over the last few years.

What about us?

It is not only debtor countries who lose out by the 'earn more, spend less' principle. The countries demanding repayment also suffer economically.

Western countries are losing out on earnings from some factory and farm produced goods because it is so much cheaper to import them from the Third World. At the same time they are not able to export equipment and other manufactured goods to Third World countries which used to be trading partners, because these countries have no money to buy them. So jobs are lost and unemployment rises.

Between 1969 and 1981 exports to the poorest countries rose steadily – by about 8 per cent a year. Between 1981 and 1988, as the debt crisis came to a head, they fell dramatically.

No jobs for the boys

Before the debt crisis broke, Europe sold about a fifth of its exports to the Third World, particularly Africa. By 1990, it was only a little more than a tenth.

If Europe had continued to expand its trade at the rate it was going in the 1980s, it would have made another $171 billion dollars by 1988. This would have meant more work and so more jobs. In total over 700,000 extra jobs would have been created by now.

Movable Markets

One key recommendation of Structural Adjustment Programmes is privatisation. Governments are encouraged to transfer as much as possible out of the public sector and into private hands. This means that many multinational companies running private businesses are welcomed in Third World countries. They are also welcomed because they generate much-needed foreign currency.

And multinationals are only too pleased to set up in poorer countries. They can pay lower wages to their employees – and laws about working hours and conditions are often less strict. So the company makes more money; jobs in the West are lost; and workers in poorer countries have to accept bad working conditions.

Sample page from the Debt Cutter's Handbook

One of my favourite quotes a year later from Ann fully validated the way in which the *Debt Cutter's Handbook* met our three objectives:

> *Government officials have been amazed at the commitment and detailed knowledge of ordinary people. 'What is going on here?' asked one surprised British treasury official. 'We are*

getting letters on pink paper with little bunches of red roses in the corner – "Dear Sir, I understand that you have not included Uganda's post cut-off-date debt… "'

4000 resource packs (one ton in total weight) were delivered to the office at the beginning of September 1996, leaving Celia little room to manoeuvre around the already cramped office, but fortunately demand was brisk and further editions were required within two years. Just as well given that the cost of design and printing was over £8,000 in addition to the editing costs.

Our communication and educational materials generated moral outrage as people came to grips with the basic facts. In the first *Debt Cutter's Handbook* we originally estimated that for every £1 given in aid, the UK received back £3 in debt repayments from poorer nations. Actually, when these figures were recalculated in 1999, it worked out as £13 given back in debt repayments for every £1 given in aid.

CHAPTER TEN

The Joys of Obtaining Funding

Funding applications seeking start-up funds were made to a number of groups during the initial year or two. Negative replies were received from Glaxo, the Co-operative Bank, Allied Dunbar, Rowntree's Reform Trust and then from the National Lotteries Charities Board (that application had been particularly time-consuming and large), all saying essentially that our application had been unsuccessful as grants were only made for work targeting beneficiaries in the UK.

Smaller applications for funding (mostly for printed materials) were made to the Evangelical Alliance, Tear Fund, Oasis Trust and Body Shop with some limited success. By January the two most hopeful remaining sources were the Tudor Trust and a private trust fund in Jersey (which Brendan was due to visit). In the meantime, we had set up bank accounts in the name of Jubilee 2000: the first a local one in South Cave, the small town where I lived; the next, a London-based one with the Co-operative Bank.

Will had offered to work on a covenant form, but not only was a charity number needed, but permission from the Inland Revenue was also required. However, pledges of £24,000 had been received from supporters – preferably to be covenanted, if and when we gained charitable status.

Every rejection letter brought lots of disappointment – so much was hanging on our need to be able to fund a small office and staff.

Tearfund's response

As I worked part-time for Tearfund, they were the obvious charity to approach for support and indeed potential 'ownership'. Some individuals proved very supportive and I was given the chance to share the 'vision' and Jubilee 2000's aims at staff prayers in the summer of 1995. This met with a lot of interest, but the official line remained cautious and requests for support and funding were not met. However, it did help to kickstart an internal discussion within Tearfund both about their response to Third World debt and to campaigning and advocacy issues in general.[4]

But Tearfund were happy to allow Tim Chester to attend our steering group meetings. And later, they proved unbelievably generous in distributing our first 'Sauda' leaflet to all their supporters – breaking all their own guidelines! Once the coalition was established, Tearfund played a very full and influential role.

They held a learning review regarding Jubilee 2000 in 2001. Here are some relevant comments:

"If Tearfund had not been involved in Jubilee 2000 then we would now be very upset... like the guy who didn't join the Beatles."

"The fact that Jubilee 2000 was successful, led to the valuing of advocacy within Tearfund."

At the end of January 1996, we received an interesting letter from the Tudor Trust. They commented that the proposal did not fall easily within their current funding priorities and they felt our "objectives were unachievable". Nevertheless, the trustees were intrigued by the campaign and our aims, and planned to discuss it at their next meeting, so Bill and I both responded to this challenge by letter. These letters obviously helped as they then requested a meeting with some of the trustees to further discuss potential support for Jubilee 2000. I was away in Uganda

---

[4] In 2001 Tearfund established an advocacy role appointing Andy Atkins to the post of Policy and Campaigns Director. I met him during his first week at work and have continued to keep in touch. I like to think that Jubilee 2000 helped to bring this important post forward.

on another research trip, so Bill, Ann and Tim Greene agreed to go along and met them in early March 1996.

Notes from this meeting indicate that the Tudor Trust trustees were impressed by Jubilee 2000's aims, strategy and progress thus far and had appreciated our detailed responses regarding how to persuade creditors to remit Third World debt. They quizzed Ann and Bill on their links, opinions and current campaigning targets. They moved on to discuss the kind of roles that a potential Coordinator would need to play, agreeing they would need to combine effective communication and media presence as well as understanding of the complexities of Third World debt. They were obviously impressed by the high quality of the patrons we had amassed. As the meeting concluded, the Trust Secretary, Roger Northcott, shared their proposals to fund a "high-calibre" Coordinator able to negotiate at an international level and their support costs, at a much higher salary than the one we were currently envisaging. *Wow!*

This offer was then confirmed following our submission of a detailed funding proposal. At the end of April 1996, Tudor Trust confirmed that they would allocate £25,000 for Ann to act as a Coordinator. They also requested a meeting with me – given that I had been the person communicating throughout but had missed the earlier meeting. I went along to their offices on 9th May 1996. It proved a fascinating meeting at their headquarters with the Secretary, Roger Northcott and two of the trustees. It was refreshing to meet with very well informed and confident financiers/trustees who were obviously quite intrigued by Jubilee 2000 and the specifics of what we were doing. The discussion centred a lot around my own involvement and the original vision. They said they liked the idea of Jubilee 2000 so much precisely because it "didn't fit anywhere"! Indeed, their interest had prompted them to move aside from their own criteria and guidelines. The meeting ended very positively, and they agreed to fund half of Ann's work so she could continue with the Debt Crisis Network but now work full time on Third World debt, focusing primarily on Jubilee 2000.

Tudor Trust were the first funder to give us their backing, and their interest and support continued throughout, for which we were hugely appreciative. Their support was crucial in enabling the campaign to move forward.

Jubilee reflections

In my 25 years at Tearfund I met many people and had many conversations, most of which have passed into the dustiest recesses of my brain's memory bank. But I can recall the moment that Isabel Carter explained gently, passionately and succinctly the vision she believed God had given to her as she had flown over Africa. I recall even more clearly that the explanation came with the challenge: what would Tearfund do to help make the vision a reality?

I have learned over the years that when thoughtful, rational people are sharing something they believe that God has told them, it is wise to give it careful thought – it doesn't happen that often. And it is even rarer that the vision is quite as bold, big and beautiful as the one that Isabel shared that day.

My immediate reaction was to realise that the vision was one of enormous global significance; so much so that not only was it much – much – bigger than Tearfund could possibly absorb or deliver, but any attempt by Tearfund to take it on would condemn it to failure. So I was circumspect, non-committal; Isabel possibly remembers it as a discouraging meeting! But I am so glad that I did release and encourage Tim Chester, Brendan Bowles and Mike Webb to get involved. For Tearfund, Jubilee 2000 came at what theologians sometimes call a kairos moment – a small reflection of the wider dynamic, the vital dimension of timing, the approach of the turn of the millennium which encouraged so many people to yearn to see it marked with something of lasting significance.

At Tearfund I had been trying to encourage the organisation to incorporate advocacy and political campaigning as part of its mainstream activity. The organisation had been outspoken on the politics of poverty in the past, not least through resources highlighting the views of leading evangelical theologian Rev. John Stott; but the outworking had been to steadily and resolutely encourage supporters to join the World Development Movement.

Now I had written a paper for the Tearfund Board putting the case for advocacy and campaigning being brought in-house and made a significant component of the active responses offered to supporters. Tim Chester had joined the staff to provide a solid research and information basis for this embryonic shift in emphasis; Jubilee 2000 provided a wonderful focus for developing this.

We circulated the first Jubilee leaflet and to the consternation of many within the organisation, encouraged supporters to make a donation; we produced educational resources for churches, and made them the focus of Tearfund Sunday. The result was not only good for Jubilee 2000 and the cause of debt relief, but also for Tearfund, and the role of advocacy and campaigning within Tearfund. After the human chain in Birmingham, and all that went with it, no one doubted the value of advocacy within Tearfund: it became a campaigning organisation.

I realised that my initial instinct was right – big visions and big issues needed joint action. Coherent coalitions were far more likely to bring significant change than random multiple campaigns promoted by so many organisations that they were effectively in competition with each other – competing for public involvement and for political attention. And significant change would only come about from long-term commitment.

That's why when the year 2000 came, Tearfund put such effort into establishing the Jubilee Debt Campaign to ensure that all the extraordinary momentum of Jubilee 2000 was not lost. We kept going on debt; we insisted that it should be part of the Make Poverty History campaign for the 2005 G8 summit, where we saw further significant progress.

My role as co-chair of the Jubilee Debt Campaign board ended many years ago now; but it is great to see it still continuing to make a significant contribution to the outworking of Isabel's vision. And I am deeply grateful for the privilege of having been one of the thousands empowered and enabled to play a small part in that on a personal level.

Stephen Rand
Stephen Rand was Communications Director
then Prayer and Campaigns Director for Tearfund
and Co-chair of Jubilee Debt Campaign

Chapter Eleven

Appointing Our First Staff

During the November 1995 steering group meeting, Tim Greene, Mike and I had put together some suggestions for job descriptions for a Coordinator and Administrator. These were discussed and amended at the meeting. It was agreed that Mike and Tim would work on developing an advert. Salary scales were discussed and compared with similar roles within Christian Aid.

At a meeting a month later in December, we agreed that though we still lacked adequate funding to offer employment, there was a desperate need to have some full-time staff. We decided to proceed in faith! Tim and Mike finalised the job descriptions and the qualities needed, and came up with a job advert. We had already missed the deadline for most magazines for January and the cost of an advert in *The Guardian* would be considerable. We decided first to go for a free mailshot to all Debt Crisis Network members and other relevant groups in December. If little or no response was forthcoming, an advert would be placed in *The Guardian* in mid-January. Mike, Tim and I agreed to handle applications and draw up a short list, since living in the same small town meant it was easy for us to discuss together.

Following this decision there began one of the most stressful periods of the campaign for me personally. It was a time when my faith in the vision I had been given was sorely tested – a time when often I was aware my faith was carrying others onwards. Now we were not just talking about plans and aims, but we were putting people's livelihoods at stake. We were advertising in faith – without yet having the means to pay salaries for more than six months – and we still lacked an office base. If we delayed, we would not only lose time but also the opportunity of using the wonderful opportunity of launching during the Debt Crisis Network's week of action – an African tour in February 1996 (bringing over five African leaders). Ann wanted our campaign to be the finale of the week, which would focus on African debt, so that we could give people something practical to go away with and put into action.

Designs for the leaflet were also now continuing in earnest with proofs circulating. The aim was to have this leaflet printed and ready for the Debt Crisis Network's week of action. In addition to the stresses of mediating between members, Mark and the designer (with strongly held views on all sides), various crucial information was still pending: charity status, a bank account, patron requests and, most crucial of all, a memorable P.O. Box address and an office base.

Nevertheless, interviews were arranged for February 1997. Several group members offered help with interviewing. Two or three trustees were to be involved in the final decision-making.

Job interviews

Job adverts for both posts were thus circulated to all the 78 groups and agencies linked to the Debt Crisis Network. Using the network provided a simple method of reaching people who were already aware of the issues, and it was free. By the end of January 1996, we had received eleven applications for the Administrator post and five for the Coordinator role and we felt this was enough to allow us to avoid the high cost of advertising in the press. Shortlisting left us with three applicants for the Coordinator role and five for the Administrator post.

Interviews were held on 14th February – once again in Christian Aid. I had rather a lot on my mind that day as I was flying out to Uganda that evening for the first of several research trips for my doctoral research (looking at how rural farmers accessed and used agricultural information). Looking back, I marvel at how we packed in the interviews. It was really disappointing on arrival that morning to find that Ann had another meeting and was unable to be part of the interviewing panel. And Cathy Brereton from USPG couldn't make it, leaving just Bill and me. But when Tim Mould heard this, he evidently persuaded Ann and she did indeed appear on schedule, much to our relief. She would be working closely with these people, so she really did need to be part of the decision-making process. Tim also pulled some internal strings and the interviews were relocated from our usual basement room to an office on the third floor, which gave a more professional feel to things.

There was little breathing space between the interviews. Two of the applicants for the Coordinator post came over as very practical and assumed that we wouldn't have any hope of achieving all our aims. But the man we appointed could see the bigger picture and came over as very organized, strategic and a careful and diplomatic negotiator. Several people met our requirements for the Administrator post and we went for someone who came with some real character. We agreed our choices in relative harmony and I managed to phone both people from the airport lounge before heading off to Kampala.

Mike had agreed to do the paperwork and follow up on references. He was also the first to hear that the person appointed as Coordinator, after much thought, had decided to turn it down as he was offered another job that week which he thought might not take over his life so much (he'd just had a new baby). I've often wondered how he reflects on that decision in hindsight!

However, this disappointing news reached me in Uganda at the same time that we heard that Tudor Trust, to our delight, had offered to fund the Coordinator post, whilst insisting that we should be going for a high-calibre person on an increased salary!

Upgrading the Coordinator role

The steering group meeting on March 15th discussed Tudor Trust's proposal for a high-level Coordinator in depth. There were concerns that such a high-profile post might present difficulties at times for the other people involved – in particular for Martin, Bill and Ann. We would have preferred a more open offer of general support that would have allowed us to spread the funding a little more. At one point during the meeting, Ann asked me, "Why don't *you* take on the Coordinator's role?" to a gentle chorus of encouragement – a suggestion which I rapidly turned down! I never sensed the vision was for me to lead, but rather to help make it happen.

James Jones, the Bishop of Hull, had echoed Tudor Trust's views, saying that it was essential for us to head-hunt the best possible person as Coordinator. He commented that if we got the right Coordinator, funding would follow.

Ann was concerned that this person would replicate her own work for the Debt Crisis Network. Tim Mould agreed to sound out members of the Debt Crisis Network about this and ask whether Jubilee 2000 could be seen as a project of the Debt Crisis Network if Ann considered a potential role within Jubilee 2000. I was asked to go back to Tudor Trust and see whether they would agree to their funding providing partial support for Ann to do more work for Jubilee 2000, alongside her current part time Debt Crisis Network work, and to ask if we could use the rest of the funding for setting up an 'International Fund' to enable our patrons, African leaders and committee members to travel and promote Jubilee 2000 on our behalf.

I hastily compiled a letter and supporting information regarding potential patrons, trustees and high-profile African leaders (Sir David Steel and Archbishop Tutu were among those mentioned) who could travel and negotiate on our behalf – to justify the establishment of an 'International Fund'. We provided two options. The first option was for Ann to work half-time on behalf of Jubilee 2000 (alongside her existing work for Debt Crisis Network) and for us to establish an 'International Fund'. The second option was for us to headhunt for a full-time high-calibre Coordinator.

We received back a detailed letter on 23rd April from Tudor Trust basically agreeing to our first preference – for Ann to work half time for Jubilee 2000 and the remaining half of her time with the Debt Crisis Network – "as long as this project takes precedence over other agendas for the time being..." This was sent in error to Bill and unfortunately took two weeks to reach me! Debt Crisis Network members were in agreement with the proposal regarding Ann's employment and after discussing this offer in detail, the trustees were happy to confirm Ann's appointment.

This brought a wonderful conclusion to a difficult few months and was a decision that yielded dividends in the years to come.

CHAPTER TWELVE

The Room with a View...

As the campaign began to grow in 1995, our need for an office base and postal address became urgent. Permission to use Christian Aid's P.O. Box address on the leaflet bought us a little time but a decision regarding an office had to be made before we could appoint staff.

The Columban Fathers generously offered us office space in Hampstead. Later Interhealth also agreed to make some space for us if needed, which had the advantage of being just a few minutes' walk away from Christian Aid. But neither seemed ideal, particularly now with Ann's commitments split between Jubilee 2000 and the Debt Crisis Network, so Tim Mould made a request for us to have office space in Christian Aid (where Debt Crisis Network was based). This was by far our preferred option and he reported back that the likelihood of office space there looked reasonably hopeful.

However, without adequate funds, Christian Aid were understandably reluctant for Jubilee 2000 staff to be based with them and come under their payroll and staff support systems. When a meeting was arranged to discuss this with Christian Aid staff after our steering group meeting on the 30th January, another bombshell exploded. Tim Mould, the Regional Director in Christian Aid, who had been wonderfully supportive and wise, stated that in order for us to open an office base within Christian Aid, we would have to provide advance assurances of £55,000 in addition to the £33,000 we already had promised, in order to cover the whole of the first year's costs. Our hearts sank. We couldn't guarantee anything approaching this. And we had people coming for interviews in two weeks. How could we possibly proceed without an office?

In the stunned silence that followed, a quiet voice spoke out. "I'll underwrite it." One of the steering group, Will Reid, a retired banker, rescued us from disaster. He and Tim Mould disappeared to sort out practical details and affidavits and we breathed again. I marvelled at God's provision.

We were able to release Will from this agreement in October 1996 when we were happily solvent and reasonably secure. And we thankfully never needed to claim any of this underwritten amount. But it was an amazing and sincere offer which completely saved the day!

'Office' is a somewhat grandiose description of what we were offered. In essence it was a 'shed' on the roof of the Christian Aid offices, used previously as a stationery store. It was light and of reasonable size but also absolutely freezing in cold weather as there was no insulation and there was a gap at floor level that allowed icy blasts to enter.

I still have a scrap of paper from March 1996 with a long list of 'things to do' in setting up the office, ordering a computer, software, printer, stationary, filing cabinets, shelving and storage cupboards. It also included arranging for a phone line to be installed and finalising a contract, salary and pension for Celia. Christian Aid staff were very helpful, but we didn't really 'fit the system' so there was a lot to organise and negotiate.

Still, Celia, our first administrator, soon made it into an efficient office, beginning work there on a part-time basis in April 1996 and on a full-time basis from June (once her current work ended). Ann tended to stay and work in the Debt Crisis Network office much of the time – which was considerably warmer!

Until our charity number came through, I was given permission to use Christian Aid's number to order a computer, software and a printer for the office. Christian Aid also provided the basic furniture needed and were very supportive of Celia, allowing free use of photocopying, printing and other office administrative support.

I remember visiting Celia a couple of weeks after she had started work. We were going through the post and it was very moving to gauge some of the public response to the leaflet. It included cheques, often quite large (some for £500, £1,000 and even one for £4,000 the day I was there), membership payments and orders for the resource packs. Will Reid become our official Treasurer in June 1996 and was wonderful in extracting gift aid repayments. It was all very encouraging. The mailbag was often pretty large and there must have been many times when Christian Aid regretted offering to share P.O. Box 100 with us.

From May 1996 onwards, things stepped up several gears. We had now got two great staff in place, an office (albeit with shortcomings), charity status, enough funding to be going along with initially, and a growing list of members and supporters. There had been a surge of interest from the leaflet and various opportunities for promotion. Now we could equip interested people with the handbooks too. We were finally able to print proper letterheaded paper and do away with the temporary letterhead based on our home address in North Humberside. At last we were able to publicise with enthusiasm and I have cuttings from various newsletters and magazines.

The total income of Jubilee 2000 from 1994-2000 was around £5,000,000. From the total debt relief promised by the G8 and the international institutions of $110 billion (£74 billion), it means that every £1 donated returned an incredible £14,800. Some investment!

Will Reid

Despite sitting 'on the fence' faith-wise, Ann wisely got well versed in the Jubilee principle and could happily interweave references to this in her presentations, particularly to churches, religious groups and organisations. In May 1996 she was invited to address the World Council of Churches at a symposium in Switzerland, called to consider preparations for their own Jubilee celebration in 1998. She wrote afterwards about how much she had enjoyed the various theological exponents relating to Jubilee and felt she had 'held her own' during her own presentation on Jubilee 2000.

In her report in October 1996, Ann wrote:

Jubilee 2000 operates from an office that is nothing more than a lean-to. The office is scarcely large enough to accommodate two people yet is now staffed with two full-timers, a part time coordinator and at least one volunteer. I am concerned that when the weather turns cold the accommodation will prove unsuitable for our workers.

We enjoy the generous support of Christian Aid, which provides us with free postage, stationery, printing and photocopying – a terrific resource.

On the basis of this cramped office, limited resources, but tremendous commitment, we have begun the slow uphill struggle to build an international campaign. The recent decisions by the World Bank and IMF have not helped our take, as both institutions tried to indicate that the problem of Third World debt had been solved...

My role began to change as well. I was no longer the person responsible for sorting out agendas, meetings and minutes with two staff now in place. I was no longer the person pushing things forward and handling funding and speaking requests. I was able to hand all this on to Celia and Ann with considerable relief. Just as well since my Ph.D. research in Uganda and Ghana was now well underway.

CHAPTER THIRTEEN

A Record-Breaking Petition

During the summer of 1996, Ann came up with the idea of a petition calling for debt cancellation. The idea was discussed during several meetings and various options were put forward regarding wording and ownership. The draft wording was widely circulated to all the members of the Debt Crisis Network and to EURODAD members in August 1996 requesting their feedback.

Feedback all proved encouraging, so the text was agreed and Wingfinger Graphics were asked to design a draft form, which was amended and finalised at the September meeting ready for launching in the spring of 1997. The original aim was for the petition to be presented to the leaders of the G7 at their 1999 summit.

Each petition needed to have our name, logo and strapline together with a clear request – a useful summary of our key campaign aims.

- We, the undersigned, believe that the start of the new millennium should be a time to give hope to the impoverished people of the world.

- To make a fresh start, we believe it right to put behind us the mistakes made by both lenders and borrowers, and to cancel the backlog of unpayable debts of the most impoverished nations.

- We call upon the leaders of lending nations to write off these debts by the year 2000. We ask them to take effective steps

to prevent such high levels of debt building up again. We look
for a new beginning to celebrate the millennium.

The petition was an idea that quickly found resonance and its scope widened – with other agencies producing their own versions for their supporters. Tearfund and Christian Aid were among the first to do this and later many others joined. Organisations saw it as a useful campaigning tool in terms of its content, its target and the opportunity it provided for campaigners to take action around it by seeking signatures. It thus became a campaigning activity that was jointly owned by numerous organisations.

One later version from Christian Aid was particularly attractive. It was mailed out as a folded A5 booklet with a candle on the front and information points regarding debt on the back – covering the main questions people tended to ask before signing the petition.

This was in the days before online petitions took off – so this remained a paper-based petition. The request and the Jubilee 2000 logo had to be clearly shown on every petition. I recommended that each form should always have 25 signatures for ease of counting them up! We used airmail paper for printing – which proved a useful and far-sighted choice as the petition rapidly became a global one! We undertook to have translations produced in the main international languages – French, Spanish and Portuguese – but later various other versions were translated.

Initially the petition forms were handled by staff in the Jubilee 2000 office. Barbara Withstandley wrote an update for supporters in January 1999:

> *The total number of petitions collected up to the end of 1998 is approximately 3 million and the total number of countries who have now sent petitions is 124. The individual petition cards for insertion into Christmas cards have proved to be very popular and hundreds have already been returned to the office. They are continuing to come in at a steady rate.*

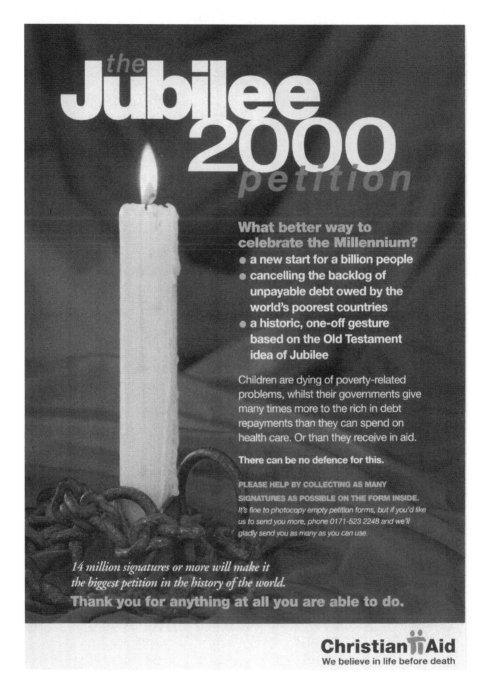

Christian Aid petition cover

Over the holiday period the variety of petition forms received continues to amaze and astound... From Christian Aid we have received thousands of signatures from India – some bearing thumbprints, and a number of their special youth forms. Health Aid MOYO sent 6,700 signatures from Tanzania. The Sacred Heart Order have their own form and it has been translated into Italian, French and Spanish...

As usual, our own Jubilee 2000 forms provide the bulk of signatures received but the reach of these forms always manages to astonish us. The English forms have come in from Australia, Bangladesh, Bolivia, the Czech Republic, Canada, Eire, Ethiopia, France, Germany, Gibraltar, Greece, Holland, India, Indonesia, Italy, Kenya, Papua New Guinea, Norway, Philippines, South Korea, Tanzania, Thailand and the USA. Some English forms which were overprinted in French, reached us from Bethlehem and Palestine and from Ramaleh in Israel. The Bethlehem forms arrived at the beginning of Christmas week, particularly appropriate we felt, with addresses such as Star of David Street etc.!

The most heartwarming was a pile of Spanish forms, some with thumbprints, from the entire population of a village in Mexico, with an official certification by the Chief of Police. Of particular significance was a pile of forms which included the signatures of the President and the entire Cabinet of the Government of Guyana.

Barbara Withstandley

I spent several Saturdays out on the streets with either the Hull Jubilee 2000 group or with members of our local World Development Group asking people to sign the form. I have memories of one day when we chained up some people from key professions in the main shopping area in Hull – a medical doctor and a teacher – to draw attention to the issue.

Many agencies agreed to include the petition with their regular mailings of newsletters. And of course the petition was brought out at every possible meeting and gathering. Slowly they began to accumulate, not just from the UK but from all around the world. As the piles began to grow, Will Reid made the generous offer to collate and count all the forms – not realising, I'm sure, just what a marathon this would prove.

He spent two years meticulously counting up the petitions as they arrived and liaising with many national campaigns around the world in the run-up to the G8 summit in Cologne.

Managing the petition – Will Reid shares his recollections

One of my tasks was to keep a tally of the signatures. And after a slow start it was amazing how men and women everywhere started to show their concern for the plight of the world's poorest people by signing our petition in ever-increasing numbers. Even in relatively poor countries, which were not on the HIPC list and with no hope of debt relief, ordinary people did not hesitate to help.

Signatures were collected in all weathers in every continent; in villages, towns, cities; on the hillsides, by the roadsides; in universities, in schools, in doctor's surgeries; at concerts, markets, carnivals; and of course even then on the Internet. A prisoner in a psychiatric wing of a Liverpool prison got all the inmates to sign; in Hiroshima, devastated by the atom bomb in 1945, thousands signed; in almost every church in the UK, it seemed, visitors found the petition on display so that they could add their signatures too. All the playing staff at Bury Football Club signed; scout troops and girl guides took up the challenge; one lady in Neath, Wales, collected an estimated 6,800 signatures. Ladies in India travelled through endless villages, day after day, collecting signatures, even where many could not write and could only show their support by signing with a fingerprint. The support was just overwhelming.

Fortunately, I didn't have count them all although I must have counted millions. We never imagined that support for the petition would reach the heights it did.

The largest contributions came from:

UK 3m, Bangladesh 2.4m, Peru 1.8m, Germany 1.2m, Spain 1m, India 0.9m, Ireland 0.9m, Brazil 0.8m, Nigeria 0.8m, Canada 0.6m, Australia, France, Japan and US all 0.5m.

And other countries which responded well above expectations were Bolivia, French Polynesia, Peru, Zambia and the Federated States of Micronesia.

One side effect of all these petitions flooding in, was that my stamp collection found a new lease of life.

The Dean family with chains in Hull

In Birmingham, May 1998, 1.5 million signatures were presented to Clare Short during the G8 summit. A year later in Cologne, June 1999, that total had swelled to over 14.7 million. Indeed, in the weeks before the Cologne summit, signatures were arriving so fast it was hard to cope with them all. But the forms were all put in a large sack and presented to Chancellor Schröder of Germany.

Tearfund UK managed to break the world record for the number of signatures obtained in one day when they collected over 225,000 signatures during the Euro elections in June. Even a seagull tried to help by making its mark!

The signatures would not have been possible without tens of thousands of people organizing and arranging for the forms to be signed. They were collected in towns and cities all around the world, during markets, carnivals and events.

In Peru, Jubilee 2000 organiser Laura Vargas worked with the Episcopal Commission for Social Action to collect an astonishing 1,850,060 signatures – which represented over 5% of Peru's population at the time!

Taking the amount of debt relief promised by the G8 in December 2000 – US$ 110 billion – this meant that each signature on the petition was worth US$5,610 (£3,740). None of us regularly sign cheques for £3,740 yet each signature, often from people who had literally nothing else to give, was worth this large sum.

Will Reid

In the end the petition broke two Guinness World Records, one for the largest global petition ever gathered (the number to beat was 21,202,193 on the partition of Korea) and another for being the most international, with 165 countries taking part. It was finally presented to Kofi Annan, UN Secretary General, in September 2000 by Bono of U2 and President Obasanjo, Nigeria, with a truly astonishing 24.3 million signatures from 160 countries!

Will Reid, who meticulously checked, sorted and counted every single signature returned on the Jubilee 2000 petition, actually disputes this often-quoted total:

I felt that I could only record 19.6 million signatures on the Jubilee 2000 petition – which still made it the largest international petition ever. Those final 4.4 million 'missing' signatures were counted by others, but I was never given any proof that this number had been verified. These final 'missing' signatures were from a multi-purpose petition which was circling round America in the last days of 2000 and which had 10 different themes – one of which was dropping the debt of the world's poorest countries. And even though they may have achieved 4.4 million signatures, would it be right to record 4.4 million as all backing Jubilee 2000?

Delivering the petitions

CHAPTER FOURTEEN

Sharing the Vision

There was a difficult delay in providing information for our first supporters in the early summer of 1996, given that the *Debt Cutter's Handbook* was not initially ready for distribution. Copies were finally ready by July and were mailed out immediately. This became a resource which met with much appreciation and facilitated the establishment of a number of small local groups around the UK.

Now we needed to continue informing and enthusing them. It was time to formalise the production of a regular quarterly newsletter. The first issue of *Jubilee 2000 News* was produced by Celia and Ann and was a simple photocopied affair on purple paper.

This first newsletter was sent out to the 94 people who had now signed up as members by August 1996. This included items on Burundi's debts and situation, a report from the recent G7 in Lyon, numerous networking items, a quiz and a poem from a Tearfund staff member – *'And we are the structurally adjusted'*. Though it lacked the attractive design of later issues, the content set the trend for all the issues that followed, mixing detailed analysis, cartoons, networking, news of local group activities and some items that could be used for local meetings and in churches.

By the time the second newsletter was ready in November, it went out to 607 people – a very rapid growth of membership. Later issues used a more professional design and were entitled *News and Action.* Instead of the issue numbers incrementing, as is usually the case, each issue instead counted down towards the end of 2000 – with the 'first' issue (No. 13 in January 1998) counting down towards Issue No. 1 in December 2000.

JUBILEE 2000
A debt-free start for a billion people

Newsletter
August 1996
Number 1

COUNTRY IN THE NEWS

Burundi

Debt and social disintegration

Below we outline some of the key economic facts about Burundi, a country that has been slowly descending into civil war. But first some background.

In July 1996 the army, led by Major Buyoya, a member of the Tutsi minority in Burundi, and former President, staged a coup, banned political parties and closed down the national parliamentary assembly.

Major Buyoya (President from 1987 until 1993) had earlier been persuaded by the international community to call the first multi-party elections in 1993. He lost the elections to President Ndadaye from the Hutu majority. Ndadaye was assassinated soon after. A failed military coup resulted in the deaths of more than 50,000 people. Since then Burundi has been sunk in a mire of ethnic conflict.

The trigger for the latest coup was the decision by ousted President Ntibantunganya to invite neighbouring governments to bring troops into Burundi and provide "security assistance". The government's Tutsi allies, particularly high-ranking officers in the army, turned on the President and Prime Minister Nduwayo, and accused them of high treason.

Major Buyoya's coup followed days later. There have been frequent reports of killings, some by Hutu rebels and others by Tutsi extremists. The number of casualties is unknown.

Key indicators:

Burundi is a land-locked country of 26,000 square miles (roughly the same size as Rwanda, but a tenth the size of Uganda). According to the latest data available (1994) the under-5 mortality rate was 163 deaths per 1000. This compares with a rate of 161 per 1000 in sub-Saharan Africa as a whole, and with the UK's under-5 mortality rate of 8 per 1000. Life expectancy at birth is 48 years (compared to the UK's 76 years). Between 1986 and 1990 military expenditure as a proportion of GNP fell from 3.5% to 2.2%. Health and education expenditure rose marginally.

Economy in reverse:

According to the Burundi Finance Ministry, the country's economy went into reverse between 1992 and mid 1993. Whereas in 1992 it had grown by 2%, for the next 18 months the economy declined by 7% It has since improved marginally.

Burundi is a country reliant on imports for essential items like fuel. Its dependence on exports of coffee and tea for raising the dollars it needs to pay off debts, means that its crisis-hit economy is far more vulnerable to sanctions and a blockade than many other nations.

Burundi's debts:

Burundi has external debts of at least $1.3 billion. The country's debt increased by 274% between 1980 and 1990, the years in which dollar revenues from their main exports - coffee and tea - fell in international markets. Exports decreased by 34% to $75 million during the period 1985 - 1993. Imports, mainly food, machinery and transport equipment rose by 15%, leaving a trade deficit of $97.9 million.

Coffee is the mainstay of the economy, providing almost 90% of the country's foreign currency earnings. After years of decline, coffee prices are rising - the effect of this has been to cushion the impact of the fall in coffee production caused by political upheaval.

In 1980 Burundi's debt was $40 per capita, but by 1995 it had risen, by conservative estimates, to $194 per capita. GNP per capita is $150 (compared to the UK's $18,060 per capita).

Burundi, which had no arrears on its debts in 1990 and 1991, now has arrears of $13 million.

77% of the total debt is owed to the World Bank, IMF and the African Development Bank.

Ann Pettifor

Sources: World Bank Debt Tables/Trade and Development Report 1995/World Credit Tables, EURODAD./Human Development Reports UNDP/The Africa Review 1996, Kogan Page and Walden Publishing./Financial Times, 8th August 1996/Observer, 7th July 1996/Independent 26th July 1996

INSIDE

Page 1

The first newsletter

'And we are the structurally adjusted'

This poem provides a useful summary of the issues around which people mobilised for Jubilee 2000: overambitious promises, government borrowing, rapidly enforced democracy (a frequent precondition for loans) and the imposition of structural adjustment by the IMF with its negative consequences for ordinary people, often cutting health facilities and school provision.

<u>And we are the structurally adjusted</u>

We are the structurally adjusted:
    They said we must work to get more from our fields
    That technology promised to bolster our yields.
    The government borrowed and made us buy spray
    And tractors with loans that it couldn't repay.
    So now we are debtors and nobody cares
    The exchange rate's gone up so we can't afford spares
    And all of our tractors are rusted
    And we are the structurally adjusted.

We are the structurally adjusted:
    They said if from tyranny you're to be freed
    Multiparty democracy's just what you need
    So we bought the whole system of parties and schemes
    And we chose ourselves leaders and voted for dreams.
    And we worked ourselves into the ground but we find
    That the money we sweated and bled for has lined
    The pockets of men we had trusted
    And we are the structurally adjusted.

We are the structurally adjusted:
    They said that our spending would have to be cut
    So the government hospital ended up shut.
    Expenditure targets were brought into line
    And the schools lost their staff but the army was fine.
    So our kids stay at home and we fear for their health,
    While the generals play with our national wealth,
    And we're sick and we're tired and disgusted
    And we are the structurally adjusted.

We are the structurally adjusted:
>They said the economy needed to grow
>Cash crops were the thing that we all had to sow
>They said they knew best so we did what they said
>We dug out the maize and grew coffee instead
>And just when we through it would all work out niche
>Some foreigner somewhere altered the price
>And now our economy's busted.

>God help us, we're structurally adjusted.

© Mike Hollow

Influential articles and books

Roger Forster of Ichthus Fellowship, an influential and thought-provoking Christian thinker, wrote a long article for Christian magazines giving a detailed explanation of the Jubilee principle and our aims. It was used in *Renewal Magazine* in October 96 with the photo of Sauda as an eye-catching start. In it he commented:

> *The heart of Jubilee 2000 is not something incidental to our Christian life and service. It is essential and fundamental to our message; a message which needs to be heard, seen and felt by the world.*

This was very helpful in spreading the word to a wider audience within the Church.

I spoke for Jubilee at a remarkable 'candle-lit vigil' on College Green, Durham in the autumn of 1999. I expected a few score at most, but found myself with an audience of well over 1,000, and with a 'pop concert-type' PA system. I had to speak for 15 minutes precisely, and stop just before the cathedral clock chimed 7.00pm, when they had arranged for all the floodlights of the cathedral and castle to be extinguished for a two minutes' silence, in recognition of the estimated 19,000 children who died each year due to debt.

David Golding
Newcastle University and Trustee of Jubilee Debt Campaign

Sauda is one day old. She already owes 30 times more than she will earn in her lifetime

A billion people are trapped. Trapped in poverty they can do nothing about. Africa now spends four times more on loan interest than on healthcare. In 1993 rich nations took back £3 in debt repayments for every £1 they gave in aid

Time to free these debtors

Jubilee 2000: giving a billion people a fresh start

The heart of Jubilee 2000 is essential and fundamental to the Christian message, says ROGER FORSTER

TWO CHALLENGES will arise for Christians who are presented with the radical objective of Jubilee 2000.

First, God is generous. Jesus was 'full of grace'. Our message is that 'by grace we are saved', but conversely we are generally selfish, niggardly and mean.

Facing up as sons to being like our Heavenly Father, namely to be like Jesus, is painful.

Releasing those who sin against us, that is forgiving them their debts, is extremely demanding. It flies in the face of our culture, even though forgiveness is the prescribed ethos of our church life.

If we have been releasing our debtors in everyday life we would find it easier to become exuberant about releasing the third world from its debt also.

Secondly, we know that we belong to a movement which is described by our founder as a 'salt and light' society.

We are at a time when those who

39

Influential article by Roger Forster
Renewal Magazine, October 1996

Peter Selby, the Bishop of Worcester, took the issue of debt very seriously, publishing an excellent book in 1997, *Grace and Mortgage,* which looked at all aspects of debt – not just Third World debt. It was his initiative that led to a presentation about Jubilee 2000 at the General Synod of the Church of England in 1998, where a resolution supporting the work and aims of Jubilee 2000 to reduce the national debt of Third World countries was adopted. The Synod also agreed to seek membership of the Jubilee 2000 Coalition and send a representative to the annual meeting.

At the end of an increasingly secular century, it has been the biblical proof and moral imagination of religion that have torched the principles of the hitherto unassailable citadels of international finance. Ann Pettifor, the director of Jubilee 2000, freely acknowledges the crucial role played by the support of evangelical Christians – it has been the financial contribution, time and energy of the churches that have given the campaign its spine...

Will Hutton
The Observer

Regional and national groupings

We were most encouraged by the spontaneous development of local groups promoting Jubilee 2000 which sprang up all around the UK. I was involved personally in the Hull group, and it proved very useful to have a listening ear on the ground and be fully aware of how such groups developed, functioned and what was most helpful to provide for them in terms of inputs. In addition, it was important to facilitate the sharing of great ideas (of which there were many arising from these local groupings) and provide practical support.

The Hull support group began somewhat tentatively in 1997 and centred initially around members of a Christian drama group called CREDO. They had taken Jubilee 2000 as their key focus and wrote a number of really good sketches. One or two of these were published in the *Debt Cutter's Handbook* and the newsletters. I engineered an invitation for them to perform at a London event, which brought them several other invitations. The Hull group with 20 or so members gained resonance from Hull's close links with Wilberforce (his home) and the anti-slavery movement. The group's activities were endorsed by Hull City Council and gained the support of the Bishop of Hull and other clergy who gave them invitations to perform drama sketches and speak in churches around the area. A permanent display for Jubilee 2000 was mounted in the William Wilberforce Museum in Hull.

CREDO drama group in action

Rt. Rev. James Jones, the Bishop of Hull; Councillor Doyle, Leader of Hull City Council; and Ian Crookham, Chief Executive of Hull City Council were among the early signees of the Jubilee 2000 petition. At the time, Councillor Doyle commented:

> *Hull City has always been identified with civil and human rights and nothing is more pressing than that of the crippling burden of debt imposed upon the world's poorest people.*

Official signings: Hull Mayor (top left);
James Jones, Bishop of Hull (top right);
Councillor Pat Doyle and Ian Crookham (below)

The Hull group were also very involved in arrangements for the Wilberforce Lecture in June 1999 as part of Hull's 700th anniversary. Bishop Desmond Tutu was the speaker at the evening lecture which was inspiring and attended by a huge crowd. He gave Jubilee 2000 plenty of positive coverage. He encouraged people by saying that 10 years ago people didn't think apartheid would end. He said:

> *We can prevail against any evil ... Jubilee 2000's efforts have revealed the immoral situation where the poor raise money to pay the debts of the rich. For goodness' sake, for God's sake, can't we follow the Jubilee principle in Leviticus and have a chance of a new beginning?*

Later he commented that debt was "like a new form of economic colonization – and we all have an obligation to recognize what is going on in the Third World". With his typical exuberance he got everyone, including the city officials on stage behind him, with their hands in the air shouting "NO!" to international debt and "YES!" to Jubilee 2000 and "YES!" to freedom.

I was a founder member of the Jubilee 2000 Tyneside committee, formed in the autumn of 1997, and on its behalf organised and promoted the regional launch of the campaign, in February 1998, at which the speaker was Adrian Lovett, the Deputy Director of the Campaign. It was the biggest regional launch in the UK – Newcastle University's Curtis Auditorium overflowed and I was forced to make more than a hundred students sit on the floor in the foyer for health and safety reasons. Happily, the address was relayed, enabling everyone to hear.

David Golding
Newcastle University and Trustee of Jubilee Debt Campaign

Hull local group and debt vigil leaflet

The petition

The Birmingham group, which was led very effectively by Audrey Miller, proved very key in the planning of the Birmingham human chain in May 1998. With their enthusiasm and local knowledge, they were a massive help both in the build up to the event and in the hosting of various events on the day.

Local ideas and innovation

A 15-foot saw-toothed shark was used for street theatre in Leeds to represent the IMF 'loan shark' touting its loans.

Students dressed in chains delivered 2,500 card chain links to the Prime Minister at 10 Downing Street.

School children planted 400 bulbs to represent the 400 Zambian children's lives that could be saved by cancelling Zambia's debt to Britain.

A giant petition form with signatures of the local football team helped encourage young people to sign in Bristol.

Pupils at St Joseph's school in Wrexham chained up their religious studies teacher and invited the local press photographer along.

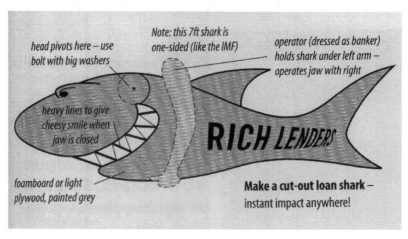

Make a cut-out shark!

A somewhat unexpected offshoot was how rapidly independent Jubilee 2000 offices were also set up around the world. There were few strings attached to how these entities managed their affairs as long as they came in under the same key aims and objectives outlined in the charter. Their inputs really broadened the supporter base and also helped to bring in the views of NGOs from the South.

One of the first was the German Jubilee campaign Erlassjahr which was launched in September 1997 and played a massive role in hosting and organising the campaigning around the G8 in Cologne during 1999. Offices were rapidly set up in Peru, India, Italy and the USA. A Jubilee 2000 Afrika campaign launched in April 1998 based in Accra, Ghana which formed a coalition with national groupings around Africa. This was later replaced in November 1999 by Jubilee South with a base in Johannesburg, South Africa. A very active Latin American and Caribbean office was set up in Honduras with a launch in January 1999 which brought in some influential international visitors. Similar enthusiasm and support were found all around the world.

German Jubilee 2000 group

It's useful to point out that the UK office lacked any funding to help these various entities. We could share our resources and allow free use of all the information we produced. We also got key resources, such as the petition, translated into several languages and sent the designed templates out for local printing in the various countries. But there was no funding to spare, so these entities were simply tapping into long-felt hurt and the desire for change.

German Jubilee 2000 leaflet

Liana Cisneros, the Latin American and Caribbean coordinator for Jubilee 2000, explained that people in Southern countries needed no education on the repercussions of international debt:

> *To them all this is obvious. During the last 20 years, they have lost access to free health care and education, thanks to IMF-directed budget cuts. The most illiterate peasant in Bolivia knows this.*

In Peru, Cisneros and her colleagues gathered 1,850,000 signatures for the Jubilee 2000 petition in five short months.

Campaigning in Peru

A number of Government and Church leaders in the South became enthusiastic promoters of our message, eloquently voicing their views on the unfairness of Third World debt.

> *The people who gave these loans knew that the money wasn't being spent wisely. Perhaps they even took their cut. Yet the ordinary people of Nigeria have to pay back these loans. This is the injustice of it all. I want Jubilee 2000 to go and preach this in Europe, American and Japan. All over the world. The burden of our debt is immoral.*
>
> *President Olusegun Obasanjo of Nigeria*

By the time the coalition was launched in October 1997, there were 3,000 UK supporters, 40 groupings around the world and Jubilee 2000 offices in five of the G7 countries.

Wearing the message

We used two ideas that supporters could wear to help spread the message and provoke discussion (and also to raise funds for Jubilee 2000). First, we produced T-shirts with a bold message – the first of which were to wear on the evening of the African Leaders Tour in February 1996. There were various later versions of this and other agencies produced their own. Our most successful idea was with lapel pins. Our first lapel pin was designed with a number 2 from which were suspended three small links in a chain. Apparently, the leaders of Jubilee 2000 in the United States urged members of the US House of Representatives and senators to wear these lapel pins at President Clinton's State of the Union address on 27th January 2000 to show their support when he spoke on debt relief:

> *In a world where over a billion people live on less than a dollar a day, we also have got to do our part in the global endeavour to reduce the debts of the poorest countries, so they can invest in education, health care and economic growth...*

Later versions in the UK used the logo and other countries developed their own adaptations.

From the outset, supporters were encouraged to take action in whatever format they felt appropriate. This was most obviously in writing letters and gathering signature for the petition, but there was no shortage of innovative ideas and responses from around the UK and further afield.

Slavery was swept away by Christian campaigners like William Wilberforce and ordinary people who brought before the government the biggest petition they had ever seen. This is our moment to bring a jubilee for the third millennium, to bring hope to millions of neighbours across the world.

Joel Edwards
Evangelical Alliance UK

And once supporters were engaged and informed about the issue of international debt, it was easy for supporting agencies to mobilise their supporters about linked issues. The devasting floods which hit Mozambique in February and March 2000 prompted Tearfund to write to their supporters with a letter from Bishop Mandlate, a key activist for the Jubilee 2000 group in Mozambique

> *Greetings from a drowning Mozambique. This is a short message to solicit your support to our call for immediate debt cancellation of Mozambique's debt. We find it very disturbing and difficult to understand that at a moment when we are busy losing lives and infrastructure, Mozambique can be expected to continue servicing her debt in the same breath that she cries for help from the world. As I am writing, we have people still on trees and on top of the roofs in many cases of shanty homes waiting for a possible rescue. Because of the lack of resources Mozambique has no capacity to deal with the situation alone. One can say that some of those people may end up falling into water because they are busy losing strength. One cannot cook on a tree even if they had food. We are counting on your support. This is the cry of the drowning people of Mozambique.*

> *Best wishes as you campaign. Shalom.*

> *Bishop Bernardino Mandlate*

Tearfund told their supporters:

> *Mozambique needs immediate and total debt cancellation to aid long-term reconstruction after the devastation caused by recent floods. However quickly international aid flows into the country, dollars are still pouring out to make payments owed on debt service.*

> *Mozambique owed $8.3 billion in 1998, and despite some debt relief last June is still paying $1.4 million a week in debt repayments. Even after further relief planned for next month, it will still pay almost $1 million each week. The long-term implications of the floods for the economy are catastrophic,*

and the Mozambican government has called for complete debt cancellation so that the money can be used instead for vital reconstruction. The World Bank is in fact increasing the debt burden, by providing its aid for the emergency in the form of a new loan.

So far, the UK is the only creditor to officially promise to cancel all the debts it is owed by Mozambique. The IMF and World Bank have proposed a temporary 'payment holiday' deferring this year's payments from Mozambique to a later date. Interest will continue to be added to the debt. This is simply not enough to give a real fresh start to Mozambique.

Tearfund encouraged its supporters to write to Mozambique's main creditors, urging them to cancel all of Mozambique's debts immediately. They listed key contacts and addresses for the World Bank, IMF and G8 leaders.

London march

CHAPTER FIFTEEN

Catching the Vision – The Development of the Coalition

As early as September 1996 (less than six months after the office opened) we were being asked whether NGOs could join Jubilee 2000. I attended a meeting of the Debt Crisis Network in autumn 1996 and was amazed to hear representatives of numerous NGOs so excited about Jubilee 2000. Also heartening (remembering my early frustrating phone calls with agencies who told me they had "done debt") was to hear that all major NGOs had now reinstated debt as a key issue, including CAFOD, Christian Aid and the World Development Movement (now known as Global Justice Now). The Church of England representatives were introducing a proposal to General Synod saying that the Church of England took Third World debt as a priority during the years approaching the millennium.

On the morning of the first Saturday in March 1997, I could have been observed to come downstairs at home looking somewhat the worse for wear! Indeed, when I went to the keypad of our alarm system, I was so stressed out I couldn't immediately remember the code! What was wrong with me? Tearfund had made Jubilee 2000, the newly launched campaign to cancel the debts of the poorest countries, its focus for 'Tearfund Sunday' – the next day, and I was really stressed by the thought of preaching about it. We'd certainly never addressed an issue like international finance, yet alone been involved in campaigning. Yet never before had I known such a compelling sense of 'The Spirit of the Lord is upon me' as when I stood in the pulpit that Sunday morning – and that occasion undoubtedly changed my life. [It is still remembered by some members of the congregation.]

David Golding
Newcastle University and Trustee of Jubilee Debt Campaign

Initially, the petition and charter had presented an ideal opportunity for other organisations to join with these key documents and put their energies behind them. This generated a good and widespread response, but in the longer term it was not enough. Agencies were frustrated that they were not part of the decision-making regarding Jubilee 2000. Humanly speaking, of course, the management group could allow ourselves to feel just a little smug that major organisations, which had regarded us as irrelevant eighteen months earlier, were now irritated that they had allowed early opportunities to join with us to pass by!

Given that we were now a registered charity and campaigning group with our own staff and office, we were now independent but, much more significantly, we were capturing the public attention and imagination. There was something about the massive aims behind Jubilee 2000 that proved hugely appealing. Once people understood what we were about, people would say, "That's crazy," but then they would pause and think again – "Well, maybe this might just be possible..." It was a big idea and the millennium warranted big thinking!

Our reluctant need to 'go it alone', because no organisation had been willing to give us substantial support, in the end proved one of the biggest factors for success and growth. We didn't 'belong' to any one agency. This had allowed us to move very fast, make some radical decisions often stepping out in faith, and develop a clear focus. Understandably, a number of agencies now wanted a piece of the action. How could they continue to promote Jubilee 2000 if they didn't have a stake in it? This situation thus led to the formation of what became a massive coalition of agencies and denominations. Early moves to develop the thinking behind establishing a coalition were laid out by Ed Mayo, and the existing board and steering group agreed to this in May 1997.

First steps towards a coalition

Ed Mayo, former Chair of Debt Crisis Network and now of the New Economics Forum, played a key role behind the scenes in developing the thinking and planning that went into the formation of the coalition. He and Sam Clarke met with the steering group, the board and with all the staff, trying to work out a smooth transition. To add to the complexities, it was also agreed on 7th July 1997 that the work of the Debt Crisis Network was to be woven into the campaigning work of the new structure.

Ed was a patient and encouraging figure, backed up ably by Sam Clarke, also with the New Economics Forum. An interim steering group was set up over the summer months to develop the coalition. He listened to everyone's viewpoints and tried to work things out in ways that held everyone together. Issues faced included who would be entitled to become members of the coalition and what inputs and rights they should expect; funding, leadership (both of the coalition and of the office), staff structure and roles. The appointment of officers for the coalition from member bodies was a key one, balancing NGO representation with local group representation. All the existing patrons would be approached and new ones considered.

I have one memo I wrote pleading that the new coalition should not spend time and money preparing a brand image for Jubilee 2000. Surely, we had already done this successfully? We were also keen to ensure that the Charter's key requests should remain largely unchanged.

The original board, still the five of us, would elect one representative to the new board and Tim Greene offered to coordinate this as he did not wish to stand. Nomination forms for all other potential members to the board of the new coalition had to be submitted in advance of the first meeting when voting would take place.

Ed was keen to inspire us, as existing board members of Jubilee 2000, with his personal vision for the coalition, and expressed it with these words in August 1997:

Jubilee 2000 is a bolt of lightning.

Lightning is a function of millions of small particles that revolve and create a combined charge that has to find something to lock onto. Those particles are always there within clouds, but only in the right conditions do them make lightning. You'd never otherwise know they were there.

Let's face it: the issues the coalition addresses have not changed in any fundamental way over the last decade. The obstacles it faces have not changed. The forces, which it can muster, have not changed. Our only hope is to bring the ingredients we have we can muster, to the point of ignition.

That means the coalition must create energy, not soak it up. It means that the coalition must generate energy in a pure not dispersed way. It means that there must be clarity of leadership. It means that there must be a cascade of action and that every action must double its own energy within the shortest period possible. It means no passengers.

A bolt of lightning is not what we are used to. It is an act of revolution. It is something that we can all think back that we achieved that in our lifetimes.

Martin Dent gathered some handing over notes for the new coalition. He wrote with feeling that...

...the small seed which we sowed at Keele in 1990, and which was so wonderfully developed, through God's Grace, by Bill, Isabel, Ann, Will and others (as well as myself), has grown into a considerable mustard tree which is, I believe, destined to become very great.

A new beginning

The final meeting of the existing Jubilee 2000 board met on 13th October 1997 – as always in Christian Aid's office – to wind up the affairs of the charity and campaigning wing. Accounts were presented and approved, and it was officially noted that we were standing aside as Directors and Trustees to allow the coalition to take things forward. We then had an informal lunch, joined by Celia, whose post was regrettably not being included in the new structure.

Farewell before lunch, 13th October
Left to right: Bill, Tim, Isabel, Will, Celia and Martin

We then proceeded to the first assembly of the new coalition which was taking place that afternoon in the Jubilee Room of the House of Commons and chaired by Michael Taylor of Christian Aid (Ed Mayo was subsequently elected as Chair at the first board meeting). We began with messages of encouragement from Archbishop Ndungane of South Africa and Susan George which were read out to us. Various people, including Ann, presented reports outlining the name, objectives, budget, the constitution and membership of the new coalition. There were 26 organisations who committed to support the coalition at that first meeting, together with eight regional groupings (including the Hull group which I belonged to). Elections to the steering committee followed with eleven places available in total. I was elected to stand as the representative trustee by the original steering group for the first year, so my involvement would continue but would be in a very different format. I remember that the Jubilee room was packed that day and there was a great sense of excitement and new beginnings.

Coalition leaflet

Membership of the coalition grew rapidly, bringing with it the potential support of up to 8 million UK members who were linked to the member organisations. By the year 2000 the coalition was supported by 110 member organisations including aid agencies, Christian denominations and trade unions. I believe that at the time it was the largest single-issue coalition. Two largely information-sharing assemblies were held each year, with annual elections to the decision-making board, which met more frequently.

Soon the coalition brought together other religious groups too, including Jewish and Islamic support. In 2000 our website featured an interview with Sahib Mustaqim Bleher, General Secretary of the Islamic Party in Britain, explaining why teachings from the Koran had influenced in deciding to support the aims of Jubilee 2000 and encourage other Muslims to do the same.

As the coalition grew, unsurprisingly tensions were often apparent. It was an unwieldy structure to manage, bringing together so many agencies, all with their own agendas to answer to. Bill and Martin found their loss of influence particularly hard but were made Vice Presidents at the first board meeting in 1997. This, however, made little difference to their frustrations in wanting to continue their commitment to the work and influence of Jubilee 2000, as decision-making, speaking opportunities and invitations all now went to others. Ann's leadership and growing influence brought huge and beneficial impact, but coalition members complained that she would lead independently whilst they often had to follow. Yet day-to-day opportunities and openings rarely wait for quarterly meetings. It's unusual for a coalition to form following a successful independent campaign – usually the coalition forms first and agrees the agenda and format of structures and staffing to carrying out their wishes. Tensions and frustrations rapidly arose, given that the campaign staff had long been used to independent decision-making. And insufficient funding was always a concern – with coalition members and supporting NGOs unwilling for Jubilee 2000 to make its own funding appeals, which would be at the expense of their own income.

Michael Randle wrote a balanced review of the coalition in 2004 noting the tensions that developed – in particular regarding funding and the sometimes fraught relationship between the secretariat and the coalition board.[5] Given the initial freedom of Jubilee 2000 to move forward, it was perhaps not surprising given that since most of the original staff remained in post, the secretariat continued to make plans and assume the board would give these their blessing. But tensions obviously abounded at times.

However, the coalition held together, not just in the UK but globally, and had a truly massive impact. Supporters were happily unaware that there were sometimes cracks in the coalition – and were able to rejoice at being part of such a fantastic body with a single purpose.

NGOs are generally in competition with each other, each fishing in the same 'pond' for supporters and funding – so it is rare for them to put the agenda of a coalition above their own agendas. Nevertheless, by and large this happened, which is why the coalition stayed together and on occasion pulled off some magnificent campaigning in unison.

---

[5] Randle, Michael (2004); *Jubilee 2000; the challenge of coalition campaigning;* Centre for the Study of Forgiveness and Reconciliation, Coventry University.

CHAPTER SIXTEEN

Amazing Events

All kinds of events occurred both in the UK and around the world as the coalition gathered impetus and influence. My recollections are a very incomplete picture, mostly of those I was either involved with or aware of through contacts and friends.

Obviously, the events in Birmingham 1998 probably feature highest. The summit in 1998 was the first time the group of global leaders met as the G8 rather than the G7 as Russia joined them. Jubilee 2000's actions had forced the issue of debt relief onto their agenda in 1998. They had never discussed it together before. But the nature of the huge coalition behind Jubilee 2000 and the size of the human chain helped make debt a key agenda of the G8 that weekend.

When I heard that Tearfund was calling for 5000 of its supporters to contribute to Jubilee 2000's 'Human Chain', during the G8 summit in May 1998, I knew I would not be able to live with myself unless I delivered one percent of them (i.e. 50 people). In fact, I filled two coaches (nearly 100). I also organised and filled two coaches for Jubilee 2000's 'Human Chain' in Cologne a year later.

David Golding
Newcastle University and Trustee of Jubilee Debt Campaign

People used their imagination and travelled to Birmingham by coracle, rickshaw and vintage trains, as well as the more usual coaches and trains. Some people walked to the summit in small groups over a period of four days. A flotilla of canal barges came from Hertfordshire. Creativity was also expressed in the different outfits worn. "Wear something red," was the instruction given – people interpreted that in a myriad of ways, including colouring their skin and hair. Human chains were first used symbolically in Birmingham but afterwards the idea followed the G8 summits around the world.

At one of the talks in St Chad's, Birmingham that morning, the CAFOD Director Julian Filochowski told the crowd they were part of a "jubilee crusade". He said:

> *Our presence is a witness, a message to our political leaders of the deep-seated, real hope and yearning in our country and beyond, for a radical millennium gesture for generous, meaningful and speedy debt cancelation. We want to give a new start to a billion of the world's poorest people as the new millennium begins.*

In St Martin's, Bull Ring, 2000 people packed the church to listen to a variety of speakers including MPs, church leaders, NGO leaders, trade union leaders and leaders from African and Asian countries talking about the consequences of debt for people in their countries. As Ann arrived to speak, she broke the news to great cheers that Tony Blair would now return in the early evening to meet with coalition representatives and discuss the G8's response.

I ran along the chain for two miles to deliver some banners in different languages to the international section of the chain. I passed gospel choirs, doctors dressed in surgeon outfits, students, dreadlocked crusties and church congregations. There were masses of banners, painted faces and samba drums. From the international part of the chain, you could see a constant thick stream of people all the way down the street, over a long pedestrian bridge and down the other side. At 3pm a wall of sound erupted along the chain forcing out spontaneous noises from cars and coaches on the road. At 03.20 our section of the chain dissolved into a spontaneous ceilidh dance led by some kilted Scots.

Nick Buxton
Communications Manager, Jubilee 2000

The petition was carried from Carrs Lane Church Centre by eight Birmingham school children, each with a box of petitions and representing a G8 country. A town crier announced their progress along the human chain together with a number of bishops. When they reached St Philip's Cathedral, they handed the petitions over to Clare Short, International Development Secretary of State, at 3.15pm. A few weeks before, Clare Short had been most complementary about the campaign: "Jubilee 2000 have done a glorious job in mobilizing support in this country and internationally for debt relief for the poorest countries." As she accepted the petition she said that the "human chain was about more than debt relief. It was a symbol against the selfishness of the 1980s and 1990s."

The human chain around Birmingham spanned 9 kilometres in length circling around the whole centre of the city and was made up of 70,000 people. They came not just from all over the UK but also from Germany, Norway, Sweden, France, the United States, Kenya, Ghana, India and elsewhere.

Later that week in Prime Minister's Question Time, Tony Blair commented:

I pay tribute to the Jubilee 2000 campaign and its dignified breaking the chain demonstration in Birmingham on Saturday. The issue is vast and complex, and it cannot be solved overnight – we have to mix realism with our idealism. ... Our view is that the most persuasive case for more debt relief is that it is only when those countries can escape the burden of their debt that they are able to develop economically.

And by way of apologizing for the disappointment generated by the lacklustre G8's communiqué, he commented:

I share some of the disappointment of Jubilee 2000 on debt restructuring. I doubt whether we will ever go far enough to

117

meet the full concerns of any group in that respect, but we would have wished to go further.

Rickshaw reminiscences

It was early 1998 and I'd been doing bits of design work for Jubilee 2000 for some time. My latest commission was to design a leaflet to encourage people to come to Birmingham to form a massive human chain around the G8 Summit that coming summer. 'We want people to come by as many different modes of transport as possible.' And that was when I remembered that I'd recently met someone from York who said he had an Indian cycle rickshaw. I tracked down the current owner of the rickshaw and headed off to York to negotiate a hire charge and arrange some riding lessons.

Several months later, a small posse of freshly trained riders set off from Leeds Town Hall pedalling the rickshaw with an attendant bevy of bikes. One of my fellow riders was the notable local eccentric and cycling legend, Tim Harberd, who had a wonderful handmade silk Jubilee 2000 banner flying from a bamboo pole at the back of his bike.

Although we were the cause of many a long tailback over the next three days as we sweated at stately speed towards Birmingham, the majority of drivers tolerated us with good grace, and many indicated support for our cause. Apart from those in Reliant Robins. For some reason, these drivers seemed to resent this threat to their dominance of three-wheeled locomotion, and more than one hurled abuse as they sped past.

On the day of the planned demo, we set off on the last leg of our journey, from Lichfield Cathedral to the centre of Birmingham. We attracted a lot of attention as we navigated flyovers, roundabouts and dual carriageways. When we finally arrived, we parked up and made our way on foot to join the crowds who were forming the chain around the city centre. There seemed to be a lot of us – and not just the usual activist types. Families were enjoying the excitement and sunshine, and there were clearly plenty of elderly people too with a passion for seeing un-payable debts cancelled.

*There was a lot of waiting around while the chain was forming –
and afterwards the crowd seemed in no hurry to disperse,
although there was nothing much to look at as we lined the
roadway: all the traffic had been excluded. Every so often, a police
car would go past, and a cheer would go up – not something I've
experienced at any other demo before or since!*

*I can't remember who it was who suggested that we take the
rickshaw round the whole route of the chain – but shortly
afterwards we found ourselves at the centre of attention and wild
cheering as we pedalled the circuit with this richly symbolic piece
of poor-world technology. It was a very heady experience – and
when we'd completed the lap, someone said, "Wow! Let's go
round again!" So we did.*

*We gave ourselves the rather grandiose title of the Jubilee 2000
Rickshaw Freedom Riders, and we even had our own anthem to
the tune of Rawhide ('Rollin', rollin', rollin'. Keep them rickshaws
rollin'. Though the debt has swollen. Rawhide!' etc.) That three-
day journey to Birmingham was the first of many debt pilgrimages
we were to make over the next few years, culminating in the
glorious 1,260-mile ride from Leeds, over the Alps, to the 2001 G8
Summit in Genoa in northern Italy. And in the meantime, we'd
learned how to mass-produce Tim's beautiful banners to maximise
the spectacle.*

Bill Phelps
Wingfinger Graphics
(who produced most of the wonderful design work for Jubilee 2000)

Lambeth Conference

Key attendees at the Lambeth Conference in July 1998 ensured that
Third World debt was firmly on the agenda and one day was set aside to
focus on the topic. In particular, Archbishop Ndungane of Cape Town
spoke out with passion and challenge:

*Our continent is experiencing a new awakening in which its
people are determined to take their destiny into their own
hands. I come to this conference as a Church leader whose*

119

jurisdiction covers countries like South Africa, Mozambique, Lesotho, Swaziland, Namibia, Angola and the Island of St. Helena. All of the countries of my jurisdiction are affected and damaged by the crisis of international debt. It is a crisis that has become of the first magnitude in the world.

We here at the Lambeth Conference have a unique opportunity to address this crisis. ... The crisis of international debt that we are debating here today is not just a matter for the poorest countries. Nor is it a matter that only affects sovereign governments. It affects all of us everywhere, all of us who have become too dependent on credit cards. It affects those of us who struggle to repay loans to pay for the very roof over our heads. And those of us who live in fear of losing our jobs, and therefore our ability to repay our debts. Those of us in hock to the loan-sharks that prey on our poorest communities. We all live in the grip of an economy which encourages over-lending and over-borrowing. An economy which drives us relentlessly into debt. But the poorest, those with very little income to depend on, are not just in the grip of this economy. They are enslaved by it. They live in bondage to their creditors.

... 'We' proclaim that the only economy that will work is one based on the beautiful vision of humanity which God in Jesus Christ came down to show us. It's a vision of love and grace, of compassion and equality. It's a vision, as the Archbishop of Canterbury reminded us, of the possibility of transformation and renewal. It's the vision of Jubilee, of the year of the Lord's favour, in which Jesus brings "good news to the poor". In which he proclaims "release to the captives and recovery of sight to the blind" and lets "the oppressed go free". It's a vision that releases the poor from the prison of indebtedness and dependent poverty. It's a vision where God's people have all that is necessary to live a human life – food, clothes, shelter, good health, and a chance to expand their opportunities through education. But it's not just a vision for the poor. It's a vision for the rich too. It is a Jubilee for the powerful, who

need a new vision of the proper use of riches, and the true value of all people. Through this vision we are called to our full humanity. So let us rejoice in this gathering, and in the unique opportunity given to our Church, to proclaim our full humanity.

Let us remember above all that we are here to give a presence and a voice to the poor. The Church can make the poor present, can bring the voice of the poor into the room, can make the poor consequential. We are perhaps the only global, national and local institution that will give a presence and a voice to the poor, will defend the poor, will fight for the poor.

... As this crisis has deepened, so poor indebted countries are increasingly transferring their tiny wealth to rich countries. They do this by paying interest, and then compound interest, on loans they have sometimes repaid several times over. They do this by using money given for aid and development to pay off debts. For every $1 that rich countries send to developing countries, $11 comes straight back in the form of repayment on debts owed to the richest countries. So wealth is trickling up from the South to the North. Countries of the South find themselves giving away, virtually free, their precious commodities, like coffee, copper, tea and sugar. This is trickle-up, not trickle-down. This is a form of economics that denies us our humanity, rich and poor alike.

We are debating this issue today because trickle-up is not working. Because enslaving the poor through debt is unjust. Because each day the poorest countries transfer $717 million, to the richest creditor countries. Because each year Africa transfers $12.5 billion to Western creditors.

... We recognise that the World Bank / IMF Initiative – HIPC – the Heavily Indebted Poor Country Initiative – which offers limited debt relief to some of the poorest countries was a historical breakthrough and a good beginning. But it is not enough. ... Outright cancellation is needed. Substantial and permanent debt relief, including outright cancellation, is a *necessary and early part of the remedy which will enable these countries to thrive.*

... Observe, my brothers and sisters, that the world is waiting for a word of hope, of encouragement. The world longs to hear good news for the poor and recovery of sight to the blind, and to be told that now is the year of the Lord's favour. What will the bishops give them? Bitter, distressing words of conflict over what it means to be human? The world already has more of that than it can bear. What the bishops can give them is one voice, a voice strong in defence of the poor, bold in contradiction to the rule of money, and full of the love of God. I invite you, my fellow bishops, to take this matter prayerfully into your own hearts. What is God calling you to say to the Church in your own country – to the members of your Diocese; to the rich and powerful in your country?

... I have a dream. That we will celebrate the birth of Christ our Lord with a truly Jubilee celebration – by the cancellation of the unbearable debts of the poorest countries. That we will give a billion people a debt-free start. That the Third Millennium will be a new beginning for the Third World. Help us realise that dream!

Following a number of passionate presentations and discussions, the Bishops all agreed to back Jubilee 2000 and their support was detailed in *Resolution 1.15 on International Debt and Economic Justice* which included this quote:

(e) The need for debt relief for the poorest nations is urgent. Children are dying, and societies are unravelling under the burden of debt. We call for negotiations to be speeded up so that the poorest nations may benefit from such cancellation by the birth of the new millennium. The imagination of many, rich and poor alike, has already been gripped by the stark simplicity of this call. This response can be harnessed for the cause of development.

Bishops from around the world at the Lambeth Conference, 1998

Jubilee clock

This was one of Ann's ideas. A digital 'Jubilee 2000 countdown' clock was built into Piccadilly Circus and launched on 6th April 1997 to mark 1,000 days before the new millennium. Free rental of the space (worth about £1 million a year) was provided courtesy of Land Securities plc. However, the coalition had to pay for the construction and installation of the clock. Will was instrumental in sorting this out. It provided a useful media focus as the days clocked down. Issues over its financing dragged on but fortunately Tudor Trust agreed that outstanding funds not used for an international statesperson could be used to cover the costs.

Elinata's talk with Gordon Brown

Gordon Brown, then Chancellor of the Exchequer, was a significant supporter of the aims of debt relief and spoke at several Jubilee 2000 events. Just at the outset of the G8 summit in Cologne where international debt was on the agenda, Gordon Brown agreed to a request from Tearfund to speak directly to a lady in Zambia; someone who was directly impacted by Third World debt. With considerable effort and technical expertise, Tearfund linked up two screens via satellite and

Internet technology, so that Gordon Brown could speak directly to Elinata Kasanga, a mother living in the isolated village of Balakasau, eastern Zambia on 17th June 1999. Zambia was a country suffering considerable economic pressure. Its external debt had more than doubled in the past 15 years, and 70% of the country were living below the poverty line (at that time US$1 per day). Elinata was a widow with seven children and could not afford to send all of them to school or to pay for medicines for her children if they were ill (fees for medical services were introduced in the 1990s by the Zambian government to help meet its obligations to foreign creditors and banks). Elinata's main source of income was to collect grass but this was becoming harder and her meagre income continued to fall; "Life is difficult for me. This is my experience. What can I do?"

Mr Brown agreed that it was wrong for her children's chance of education and health to be dependent on her gathering a good harvest and that he hoped that "every child should have free education in Africa, and we must have healthcare systems which give free healthcare to children and families". He told her that he hoped the G7 leaders would shortly make a historic decision for the millennium by reducing the debt burden of the poorest countries by two thirds. This conversation was broadcast to an audience around the world shortly afterwards via the Tearfund website.

G8 summit in Cologne 1999

In June 1999 Jubilee protesters descended on Cologne, Germany over the weekend of the G8 summit on 19-20th June. This time round, the coalition were more prepared for a massive surge of public interest, though obviously the planning needed to be even more organized given the distances involved and the need to provide accommodation. We were now living in Bridgnorth, Shropshire. I gulped and decided to book a coach and accommodation for 55 people to attend but in fact had little problem in filling the coach. The coalition were able to arrange a really good deal with Harry Weeks Travel and Travelscope at £79 for all travel and two nights' accommodation which included a donation of £5 for Jubilee 2000! Fortunately, there was no shortage of people in the UK keen to pay for the travel, accommodation (in hotels and guest houses along the Rhine) and the chance to register our concerns at another G8 summit.

We stayed in a pretty little town on the banks of the Rhine and enjoyed exploring and a good meal on the Friday evening. On Saturday June 19th, the second day of the G8 summit, we travelled by extremely efficient trains into the centre of Cologne to join with 50,000 other Jubilee 2000 supporters from all over Europe and a few from even farther afield. The local trains filled up with other supporters and I remember exchanging my British Jubilee 2000 pin badge with one belonging to a Swedish lady – such was the warmth and sense of unity! There was a united service during the morning in the beautiful cathedral.

Popular purchases were the rainbow scarfs produced by Erlassjahr, the German Jubilee 2000 group. Again, there was the formation of a human chain looping over the roads, bridges and along the banks of the river Rhine. Once again, the sun poured down. Afterwards the gathering morphed into a wonderful open-air dancing session, with great world music and thousands of relaxed campaigners joining in. This time round we had something to celebrate following the announcement the day before of the Cologne Debt Initiative.

Cologne – Rhine barge

Bridgnorth group in Cologne

In Cologne: Isabel and Ray Gill (left);
Naomi and Ray (middle); Betty Carey (right)

Sign in Cologne

Cologne 1999 Debt Initiative

This pledged US$100 billion worth of debt cancellation (out of the total of $260 billion owed) and the speeding up the HIPC process so that 25 out of the 40 most indebted countries would receive debt relief by the end of the year 2000. Though the US$100 billion sounded impressive, only US$16 billion was actually new money, as the rest had already been promised but not released via HIPC, the cancelling of aid loans in 1978 and the cancelling of bilateral debts in 1994 (the Naples terms).

This wasn't anywhere near what Jubilee 2000 were asking for and so, as planned, a delegation including Ann and Bono met with the German Chancellor Gerhard Schröder to present their request for deeper action and present the petition, which by now numbered 17 million signatures. Gordon Brown also expressed a cautious desire to see more action:

We greatly welcome the contribution the churches and non-governmental organisations have already made to securing public support for reform, and we support their desire to

127

pursue the issues further. The package is a good one – but it is not the ceiling of our ambitions.

I can still remember carrying box after box of petitions from a boat to the location of the G8 leaders meeting in Cologne, Germany, in 1999. I was one of a chain gang, linked by shackles on our ankles, symbolising the message of the petition that the chains of debt would be broken. It had been signed by 17 million people from over 160 countries – the world's first global campaign. 233,000 signed the petition on European Election day in Britain.

The petition reinforced the impact of the human chain created by 70,000 campaigners that welcomed the G8 leaders to Birmingham in 1998. It was peaceful, cheerful, determined and unprecedented – and it made a difference.

The world has been changed. Poverty is on the world's agenda as it never has been before. There is an expectation that world leaders will act on behalf of people in need. In 2000 at a special session of the United Nations the world's countries adopted the Millennium Development Goals, promising action to halve world poverty by 2015.

Stephen Rand
Stephen Rand was Communications Director
then Prayer and Campaigns Director for Tearfund
and Co-chair of Jubilee Debt Campaign

Following the Cologne event, there was a real concern that many supporters would relax and feel that their work was done, so there was a flurry of reports circulated to unpack the details.

The London Chain

Partly in response to the inaccessibility of the G8 summit in 2000 – to be held (deliberately?) on a remote Japanese island, a London-based event was planned a month earlier. This was held on 13th June 2000 along the banks of the Thames following a midday rally in Trafalgar Square. Once again there was a human chain and river spectacular along the Thames South Bank which began at 2pm. For the first time, I wasn't part of the chain, having been invited as an 'honoured guest' for lunch and to watch the spectacle from the balcony of the South Bank Centre.

March in London

London demonstration

The July G8 summit was held on the remote southern Japanese island of Okinawa in 2000. Few campaigners were able to travel there but instead prayer vigils and 'summit watches' were held around the world. Tearfund was among several agencies who produced a service outline as part of the 'summit watch'. We held an ecumenical summit watch in Bridgnorth on 21st July and it was a positive experience, helping to make up a little for missing the opportunity to attend in person. There were over 600 similar summit watches elsewhere in the UK and farther afield. CAFOD encouraged their supporters to 'send themselves' to Japan by sticking their photo on a postcard and signing a letter to the Japanese Prime Minister asking him to use his position as host of the G8 summit to make a real difference to millions of lives.

The last day of the summit was 23rd July 2000 – and that was a day when history could have been made by the G8 members, and we knew we had the support of several of the country leaders. However, the general consensus was that the G8 failed to take any new steps on debt cancellation in Okinawa and even failed to make good their promises from Cologne the previous year. And so the final focus moved to the IMF and World Bank meetings in September in Prague with just 100 days remaining of the Jubilee year.

Send yourself to Japan, CAFOD

Global Summit Watch (Christian Aid)

Global Summit Watch (coalition)

Lambeth degrees

A completely unexpected joy was the awarding of Lambeth degrees for the four co-founders of Jubilee 2000 (Martin, Bill, Ann and me) by the Archbishop of Canterbury, George Carey in July 2001. He had commented in his millennium message:

> *Jubilee 2000 is a moral challenge – to the world, to every nation and to us. I urge us all to be informed ... and unite in a campaign that might just set these captives free.*

Lambeth degrees are a historic anomaly dating back to the 16th century allowing the Archbishop of Canterbury to personally award Oxford University degrees. This privilege is generally made to a small group of church dignitaries each year. However, George Carey was sincerely moved by the work of Jubilee 2000 and the way in which it had galvanised church action in support of justice and so he made the personal decision to award the degree of Master of Letters to Bill, Martin, Ann and me for our work in founding and establishing Jubilee 2000. It was a highly appropriate choice of degree given the innumerable letters we had all written in the cause!

In 1533, partly because outbreaks of plague often prevented university candidates in Oxford and Cambridge from completing their degrees, an Ecclesiastical Licences Act gave the Archbishop of Canterbury the power to grant academic degrees (previously only the Pope could do this). The Archbishop could override the requirements of the universities and simply award academic degrees without examination when it was felt that candidates had met all the academic requirements. By one of the quirks of British law, this right remains. Lambeth degrees are actually academic degrees (linked to Oxford University) and can only be awarded by the current Archbishop. They are usually given in appreciation of distinguished service to the Church.

And so, on a glorious hot sunny July day, Mike and I, with our three youngsters, met up in St James' Park with Tim Greene and his wife Diana, and our previous vicar, Revd David Bailey, and his wife Katherine for a relaxed picnic lunch. These were all close friends from Yorkshire who had stood with me along every step of the rocky first two years, and thus my choice of guests. We sauntered across Westminster Bridge and were welcomed as honoured guests into Lambeth Palace. I was syphoned off to be robed up – and to greet Ann, Martin and Bill with delight.

Lambeth group
Left to right: Martin, Ann, George Carey, Isabel and Bill

We then filed through to attend a somewhat archaic but meaningful ceremony in the historic and atmospheric Lambeth Chapel. Each degree was personally awarded by George Carey as we knelt and held the seal at the bottom of the large and handwritten degree (since it was during the Foot and Mouth epidemic, the vellum used was imported goat skin rather than the usual British calf skin). I have mine framed! Afterwards we enjoyed a relaxed reception in a fine room within the Palace with wine and delicious nibbles, and posed for photos with the Archbishop. George Carey was a delightful host and really interested to talk with each of us about our personal reflections regarding Jubilee 2000. It was also really good to be reunited with Martin, Bill and Ann.

There was a particularly moving and unexpected reunion during the reception with the Bishop of Gulu, Uganda, the Rt. Rev. Nelson Onono-Onweng and his wife Brenda. They 'just happened' to have recently arrived in the UK as part of a visit with link dioceses and speaking engagements, prior to attending the General Synod of the Church of England later that year. During their introduction at Lambeth, he had recognised my name and asked for permission to attend the ceremony. I had stayed with this wonderful couple on my first doctoral research visit to Uganda in 1996 where they had pointed out the damage to their concrete floor saying quietly, "This was the bullet which shot and killed our son, fired by the Lord's Resistance Army last year during the bitter and ongoing civil unrest in northern Uganda."

Ugandan friends in Lambeth

You may find our son's memories of the day amusing (he was 17 at the time):

One of the highlights for us as a family was when we all trooped down to London to see Mum receive her posh degree from Lambeth Palace for services to Jubilee 2000. It was a pretty amazing day, strange ceremony – half very informal, the other half archaic in Latin. She now has her degree, handwritten on goat vellum, no less; must get it framed before someone spills coffee on it. Afterwards there were loads of people standing around talking, too polite to eat, or too oblivious to notice the large piles of food and drink laid out on tables. Drifting from one side of the hall to another, I skilfully pretended that I was aiming to join someone on the opposite side of the room, thus minimising the possibility of anyone actually starting a conversation with me. By repeating the procedure for a good hour, I managed to consume a large quantity of food and feel suitably ill.

A final amusing recollection was to discover that, somewhat bafflingly, I was listed as one of Premier Radio's 60 most influential Christians[6] – a list prepared for the Queen's Diamond Jubilee in 2012. I received no communication or questions regarding this and only found out belatedly that I was on the list through a colleague working at Tearfund!

---

[6] *www.christiantoday.com/article/the.60.most.influential.christians/29592.htm*

CHAPTER SEVENTEEN

Letting Go

For me personally, standing aside generally proved very easy. The vision and the 'burden' of establishing Jubilee 2000 had come at a particularly busy time of life with three teenage children, work with Tearfund that was growing and becoming ever more fulfilling, and the additional self-made pressures of doing a part-time Ph.D. which involved field work in Uganda and Ghana. In the wonderful way that God can provide, family life carried on relatively serenely throughout 1995-1998 despite all the stresses and pressures that Jubilee 2000 brought and which tended to fill all available 'spare time'.

Likewise, the research and fieldwork for the Ph.D. proved wonderfully fulfilling and productive. But reading and reflection for my studies undoubtedly suffered, and as I entered the analysis and writing-up phase, I'm not sure I could have coped if I was still 'carrying' so much of the ongoing work for Jubilee 2000.

I remained on the coalition board for the first year and it was ably chaired by Ed Mayo. I made a few useful interventions such as pleading for the retention of the existing logo, strapline and charter rather than trying to reinvent the wheel, and insisting that other related issues such as trade should not be tagged onto a single-issue campaign. Unlike other board members, I didn't have a large organization to represent and influence. At the end of the year, I felt suitably reassured that things were going forward well and were being ably managed by competent and committed people, so I decided it was time to stand down at the next elections.

Visits to the office (which in the meantime had moved from Christian Aid to nearby Remington Street) were a joy – it was such a hive of productive activity as the campaign spread globally. Staff numbers grew, as did the number of wonderful volunteers. People put in ridiculous overtime (always unclaimed) at busy times. I was kept well informed of key events and Ann continued to send her reports. Yes, I admit to various pangs at times (particularly regarding speaking opportunities) but generally felt a great sense of relief. I had never claimed expertise in the complex arena of the negotiations surrounding debt cancellation and it was wonderful to see the growing confidence and reach of staff and coalition members. My role had always been to facilitate the formation and early development of the movement – to help build firm foundations with others. The anticipation of the year 2000 continued.

CHAPTER EIGHTEEN

Celebrate the Achievements

People power

The empowerment of millions of ordinary people was one of Jubilee 2000's greatest achievements. By equipping people with clear and understandable facts and inspiring them with a vision that might just be possible, millions responded to the challenge, many involving themselves in advocacy and campaigning for the very first time. The movement brought the birth of political awareness and confidence in campaigning for many thousands of 'ordinary' people

In February 2000, Tearfund held a learning review about Jubilee 2000 to capture the lessons learned for future use. In conclusion it commented:

The success of Jubilee 2000 in achieving its objectives will have a more profound effect on reducing world poverty than anything Tearfund has achieved in the past 25 years or will in the next 25!

When we began this campaign, there was widespread scepticism that we could educate and brief a mass campaign on the complexities of debt – and maintain accuracy and integrity ... one of my lasting memories is of the Treasury official who complained to me about the number of letters he received from Jubilee 2000 supporters. They were well informed, he said, "...too damn well informed!" ... He was particularly struck by a letter challenging the Treasury's assertion that Uganda had had massive debt relief from her last Paris Club rescheduling – and pointing out that only Uganda's pre-cut-off date debt had been included. "The letter," he said, "was written on pink notepaper with a little posy of roses in the corner! Who are these people?"

Ann Pettifor
The world will never be the same, 2000

Political impact

In September 1999, President Bill Clinton made a sensational announcement at the close of the meetings of the IMF and World Bank in Washington:

I am directing my administration to make it possible to forgive 100% of the debt these countries owe to the US when needed to help them finance basic needs, and when the money will be used to do so. I don't believe we can possibly agree to the idea that these nations, which are so terribly poor, should always be that way.

Clinton continued saying countries should not have to choose between paying debt interest and "investing in their children's health and education". At the time, the total debt owed to the US by the poorest countries was $6 billion.

Clinton paid Jubilee 2000 a great compliment, saying:

It's given us a coalition that I would give anything to see formed around other issues, and issues here at home – anything. It could change the nature of the whole political debate in America because of something they did together that they all believe so deeply in.

This positive stance was a response to considerable campaigning efforts by Jubilee 2000 campaigners within the US and by personal representations made to Clinton by U2's Bono, Bobby Shriver and Adrian Lovett, Deputy Director of the UK Jubilee 2000 Coalition

After weeks of tough negotiations, the US Congress finally approved a budget that provided the funding to meet President Clinton's pledge to cancel 100% of their debt. $123 million was allocated by the Congress to fund debt cancellation. The debts considered eligible for cancellation were those incurred before the date of the Cologne G7 Summit. We hoped this commitment would intensify the pressure on other countries to do the same.

Part of an article written by Adrian Lovett, Jubilee 2000 UK

As part of the announcement of America's cancellation of debt, President Bill Clinton wrote a letter to religious leaders:

As we reflect on our own bounty we must not forget that 1.3 billion people around the world survive on less than a dollar a day, or that nearly 40 million people a year die of hunger. For many developing countries, a major barrier to progress is debt owed to other countries and to international institutions. This excessive debt can stifle growth and drain resources needed to meet basic human needs such as food, clean water, and shelter. Simply put, unsustainable debt is helping to keep too many poor countries and poor people in poverty ...

I am pleased that we have reached an agreement with Congress to fund our participation in an international plan that will help lift the burden of debt from half a billion people in the world's poorest countries ...

I would like to extend my heartfelt thanks to the many people of faith who have worked so hard to help us reach this important agreement. More work lies ahead, but it is an important first step. Your faith and your leadership remind us of what we can do together to strengthen communities ...

Sincerely, William Jefferson Clinton

Regrettably this key focus by the US towards debt relief shifted towards the end of the year 2000. In September 2000 the breakdown of the Oslo peace process and the rapid and violent deterioration of the Israeli-Palestinian conflict meant that the US focus and President Clinton's focus shifted to new peace initiatives in Israel and Palestine, and away from moving forward the debt relief process. In hindsight this was probably one of the main reasons for the lack of any kind of final gesture for the new millennium on debt relief by the G8.

Celebrity support

Bono, lead singer of U2, brought the power of celebrity to the Jubilee 2000 campaigning. He spent a lot of time meeting with world leaders and became well-briefed and passionate about the issue of debt cancellation. He had tea with Tony Blair, earnest discussion with US Senator Orin Hatch and paid a visit to the Vatican where he exchanged his sunglasses for white rosary beads with the Pope. He brought plenty of media coverage for the campaign, which added considerably to the political pressure for change.

In February 1999, Jubilee 2000 was featured at the Brit Awards – reaching a new audience through the power of celebrity with both Bono and Mohammed Ali, Jubilee 2000's international ambassador, speaking. The next day Bono had an article published in *The Guardian* outlining his support for debt cancellation noting:

> *Both sides are to blame. There's been a mix of bad lending, bad borrowing, bad economics and bad luck. Jubilee 2000 says, write off those unpayable debts in the year 2000, under an open, fair and transparent process. Put in place a new discipline for lending and borrowing to stop the debts building up again. I'm with Jubilee 2000.*
>
> *The millennium is a key moment in time. We have to grasp that moment. It is not a time for factions, for narrow sects or ideological crusades. Jubilee 2000 is none of those things. Jubilee 2000 is bipartisan. It is broad, inclusive and international. It is emerging as a fresh convergence of differing groups. Including conservative elements, recognising the rule of money-lenders has gone too far.*

He continued:

> *Making a lot of noise is something musicians do well. Florescence you could call it. We see a chance here, for an idea*

that will give not just the millennium some meaning, but also our generation.[7]

And Bono certainly honoured that. He did indeed make a lot of very effective noise on behalf of Jubilee 2000. And his rock musician celebrity status no doubt opened doors that would otherwise have remained closed – notably meeting with both Bill Clinton and Pope John Paul II during 1999. The pope gave his blessing to the idea of a Jubilee year to cancel international debt and his support for this continued during 2000, alerting many Catholics to the aims of Jubilee 2000.

Cancelling debt is a bit like climbing Everest. But that's maybe what the world needs at the end of 1999 – an Everest to climb. There's no honour, though, in climbing halfway up Everest.

Bono

Media support

The press were generally balanced and supportive in their coverage of Jubilee 2000. About 3,000 journalists were there to record the events of that momentous day in Birmingham and created a considerable media uproar – all of which added to the pressure on the G8 leaders to be seen to respond meaningfully.

The Guardian was particularly supportive in drawing attention to the issues. Here is one of their editorials reflecting back in June 2001:

Jubilee 2000 has been astonishingly successful in mobilizing mass support. In Birmingham and Cologne during the G8 meetings, the campaign got thousands of protesters onto the streets in what became the biggest international movement since anti-apartheid. Thousands of activists across the world have collected signatures and fingerprints in tiny villages, sprawling shanty towns and the heart of middle-England parishes. A remarkable coalition of the prosperous and the poor has rallied around a simple and ancient ideal of Jubilee

---

[7] *The Guardian*, February 16, 1999

for the year 2000. Perhaps its greatest achievement is a mass education campaign, explaining the complex world financial system to peasants and Western office workers alike.

2000 pence for 2000 years.

For many years, the world's poorest countries have been crippled by spiralling debts - debts which deprive those countries' people of basic resources like health care, education and water. While the rich countries get richer on the profits of these debts, the side-effects of the debt affect us all - through environmental damage, growth in the drug trade and reduced international trade. Today's special supplement on the international debt crisis has been produced by the Guardian and Jubilee 2000, a coalition of more than 70 organisations who believe that enough is enough, and that now is the time to cancel the unpayable debts of the poorest countries. Having already forced the issue on to the G8 Summit agenda, they are now mobilising people who realise the need to mark the millennium in a meaningful and positive way - people like you. .

To mark the approach of the year 2000, Jubilee 2000 is collecting individual donations of 2000 pence, just 1p for each year of the millennium. If you are interested in joining the coalition pledge to push for the cancellation of unpayable debt of the poorest countries, send for a Guardian/Jubilee 2000 Action Pack. Each pack contains information on what you can do to help the campaign, including newsletters, petition forms and ideas for action.

Simply write to the Guardian/Jubilee 2000 at PO Box 16630, London, N1 7WF, enclosing a cheque for £30 (a £20 donation plus £10 joining fee) made payable to Jubilee 2000, or call 0870 6060 203 (calls charged at national rates). Larger donations are, of course, greatly appreciated.

JUBILEE 2000

Supported by
*The***Guardian**

☐ **Yes,** let's cancel Third World debt and give the world's poorest countries a glimmer of hope.

NAME

ADDRESS

Please send this coupon to Jubilee 2000 Coalition, PO Box 10, London NW10 7WY. If you'd like to give further help, please enclose a cheque made payable to Jubilee 2000 Coalition or Freefone 0800 3281 268 for credit card donations.

JUBILEE 2000 COALITION
A debt-free start for a billion people.

☐ **No,** let's make the lazy Ethiopian spongers pay back the £7 billion they owe us.

NAME

ADDRESS

THE WORLD POWERS
It's our money and we want it back.

Parts of an 8-page advertisement in The Guardian

Marking the Millennium

In his budget speech on 17th March 1998, Gordon Brown noted:

I want the millennium to be remembered not just nationally but internationally for the redemption of debt and the reduction of world poverty.

We advocated a celebration focused on social justice and meeting the needs of others. However, to mark the millennium in the UK, our leaders chose to set up the National Lottery and build the millennium dome at vast expense, which rapidly became a white elephant. How different was the celebration that Jubilee 2000 envisaged of a new start for the poor.

Bob Geldof had an article published in *The Telegraph,* 14th December 1999:

As Jubilee 2000, the mass movement for total cancellation of the un-payable debt by January 1st … argues, the time is now. Because if not now, when? This country needs something to mark this arbitrary date in the next couple of weeks.

There is a level of expectation that a thousand domes are not big enough to fill or contain. … I utterly believe that the cancellation of debt bondage will be as profound in its consequences as the abolition of slavery. Tony, go on, be Pitt the Younger – do this thing. You are the man and now is the time.

The article sparked numerous letters in response, mostly negative!

Debt cancellation

The original Heavily Indebted Poor Countries (HIPC) initiative announced in 1996 by the IMF and World Bank required a country to complete six years of structural adjustment before it could benefit from debt cancellation. Under these terms only four countries were likely to benefit by the end of 2000. Jubilee 2000 petitioned hard for this process to be considerably improved. The enhanced HIPC process agreed in 1999 (and announced at the Cologne G8 summit in July) speeded up the process, widened the entry requirements and enabled more countries (33) to enter. It strengthened the focus on poverty reduction and social policies trying to avert the likelihood of future unsustainable debt. It also made available an additional $27 billion in debt relief.

However, this enhanced HIPC process still did not go far enough, and by way of underlining this, the US, the UK and Canada all pledged to cancel 100% of bilateral debt owed by countries within the HIPC process by the end of 1999. By the end of 2000, 20 countries had begun to see some debt relief under the HIPC initiative. Other lender countries also cancelled debts owed following the damage from Hurricane Mitch in Central America in late 1998 and by Mozambique following devastating floods in early 2000.

However, only the UK had agreed to 100% debt relief and cancelled repayments from all HIPC countries.

Changed lives

It is estimated that 52 million children today in the developing world can trace their education to Jubilee 2000 and debt cancellation.

Will Reid's website Just 1 World

Uganda was one of the few countries to benefit from debt relief through the initial HIPC (Highly Indebted Poor Countries) initiative in 1998. But the debt relief did not go far enough and within a year, after the price of coffee fell, donor funding for Uganda's debt payments to the World Bank also stopped and so the misery continued. However, by the year 2000, Uganda was one of the first countries to submit and have approved its Poverty Reduction Strategy Paper, allowing the country to benefit from debt relief under the new enhanced HIPC Debt Relief Initiative, providing faster and more effective debt relief and poverty reduction. Their debt burden was reduced by about 42% and within a year Uganda was benefitting from savings of around $90 million each year on its foreign debts. The government established a Poverty Action Fund to ensure funds channelled into primary school education, health services, and water and sanitation provision were ring-fenced.

The Uganda Debt Network reported in March 1999 that some 3,600 classrooms and 7 teacher-training colleges had been built. These initial improvements benefitted about 6 million children, doubling the number in primary schools and enabling an extra 3.6 million children to attend school. The healthcare budget was boosted by 270% and over 2 million people gained access to clean water.

Other debts cancelled through the HIPC process brought some genuine and immediate benefits including free primary schooling in Zambia, Tanzania and Malawi and health benefits including free immunisations for children in Mozambique and increased spending on HIV prevention.

Debt relief: the benefits for education

An extract from a presentation made to the Jubilee Debt Campaign in 2004 by President Benjamin Mkapa of Tanzania:

When I became President of Tanzania in 1995, our country was witnessing a serious deterioration of social services and a debt burden that was exceedingly high and unsustainable.

In the 1970s Tanzania had built an extensive education system. By the middle of the 1990s much of this infrastructure was in a state of disrepair. Enrolment in primary schools had fallen to 77%. One of my first priorities was to increase government support and to ask for debt relief. Jubilee 2000 was a great partner in this. In 2001 Tanzania was granted substantial debt relief, and this was all directed into supporting education and health. Two years later we reviewed progress in education. We could report that:

- *32,000 new classrooms and 7,500 teacher homes had been built;*
- *1,000 new primary schools had been built;*
- *the primary school population had increased by 50% with equal numbers of girls and boys;*
- *enrolment had increased from 59% to 89%;*
- *in primary schools there were now text books for every three pupils instead of for every eight pupils;*

- *the pass rate for the primary school leaving exam had risen from 22% to 40%;*

- *12,000 school committees had been trained.*

All this after just two years of adequate funding! At this rate we believe that Tanzania can achieve MDG 2 in 2006, nine years ahead of the UN target in 2015.

Achievements in summary

By the end of 2000 the Jubilee 2000 coalition had:

- 110 organisations registered as members;
- gained promises for $110 billion of debt to be written off;
- enabled 20 countries to benefit from some debt relief;
- gathered a petition signed by 24 million people from 160 countries;
- links to 69 independent Jubilee 2000 offices and coalitions around the world;
- totally changed the thinking of the international financial systems on Third World debt;
- inspired a new generation of millions of activists around the world.

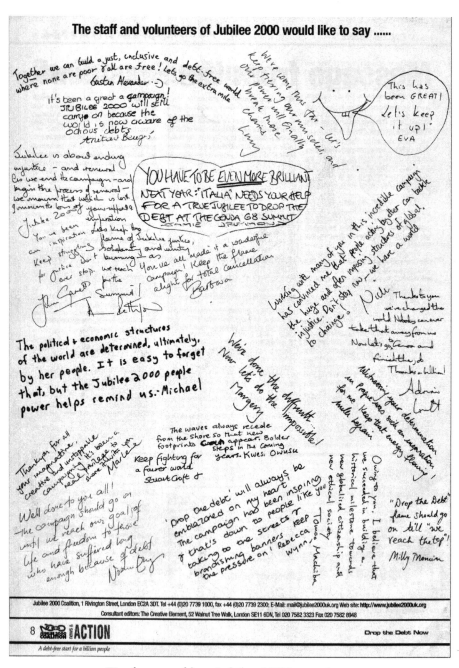

Final page of last Jubilee 2000 newsletter

CHAPTER NINETEEN

New Beginnings

From the outset we had been clear that the campaign should end by the end of the year 2000. This was written into staff contracts too. Many people were concerned and unhappy about this. However, there is no doubt that establishing a time-limited campaign meant that staff and volunteers alike were able to give it their all because they knew it would end. Coalition member organisations could give generous support knowing there was an end point when they could focus on other issues. In addition, politicians found it easier to respond to the millennial nature of our demands – this was a one-off request, not an ongoing and open-ended demand.

Ann Pettifor summarised the argument in favour of the 'short-life' campaign:

> *A short-life campaign would not be draining, we hoped; and it would set a limit on the efforts needed. Furthermore, it would give tremendous focus – and harness energies, drawing on all the hopes and aspirations of a new millennium. Above all, it would place great pressure on foot-dragging creditors to end the decades-old debt crisis, and resolve it by the year 2000.*

Jubilee 2000 remained true to its key aim. Mark Greene gave good advice when he warned us that if successful, there would be a great temptation to draw in other linked issues. Our clear charter (which was adopted by the coalition) meant that this was resisted, despite requests to do so.

151

Because we were focused on one issue and planned to end at the end of 2000, people were free to be really outspoken. There was no plan to build up a major long-term agency which would need to be careful about its future image.

But there was considerable anger and unhappiness about the winding up of such an incredibly successful coalition. It had brought together effective advocacy campaigning not just within UK civil society, but within an astonishingly broad global coalition.

Jubilee South was particularly unhappy about the year 2000 deadline. In many ways it felt betrayed by the ending of the UK campaign. And there were many very valid concerns as well – the debt issue had not been resolved in the way we had all hoped. However, the thinking about Third World debt had certainly changed. The rhetoric from governments now acknowledged that Third World debt was an outstanding issue that had to be sorted out – and indeed a huge amount of debt was already written off (£74 billion or US$110 billion was the total promised by the G8 and other international institutions by the end of 2000).

A final Jubilee 2000 public meeting and rally were held on 2nd December 2000 in Westminster, London. Gordon Brown (his own mother had pestered him about debt relief) made a historic announcement saying that Britain had now ceased to benefit from debt service payments from all 41 HIPC countries.

Stephen Rand, Communications Director of Tearfund and a board member of the coalition, spoke warmly of some of the achievements of the coalition and Jubilee 2000 at this closing event:

> *When the campaign started it was against a background of the failure of previous campaign efforts on debt to make much headway; the issue was thought to be too complicated – and the international financial institutions too impregnable – for a successful public campaign. There was serious debate as to whether the cancellation of debt was a desirable objective.*
>
> *Jubilee 2000 has changed this situation dramatically. Public opinion has been significantly informed, changed and mobilised in support of the campaign. ... This has in turn interacted with and informed economic opinion and political*

realities, to the extent that the question is no longer whether debt should be cancelled, but only how and when.

The UK Coalition has also encouraged the development of the Jubilee 2000 vision around the world, as it has been taken up by existing and new expressions of civil society in countries of both North and South.

Stephen mused over whether it was right for the coalition to close despite numerous calls for it to continue but concluded:

For me, one of the strongest reasons for closure was that the Coalition was founded on that basis. The world is full of organisations that have not known when to close. To change a longstanding commitment to close risked the credibility of the original commitment, and creating something that could limp on indefinitely rather than close effectively and hand on the baton. It is also important to realise that the Coalition has also been funded on this basis. ... In addition, the staff of Jubilee 2000 have worked with extraordinary commitment and effort, knowing when the end was due. Many of them want to continue; but many of them are also close to exhaustion.

And end it did. The London offices were taken apart and all staff knew their work was coming to an end. They ended with a great party a week before Christmas 2000. As the office officially closed, an Interim Steering Group was established by coalition members to oversee the process of launching a successor organisation to Jubilee 2000 in the UK which took the name of Jubilee Debt Campaign.

Ongoing work

A number of the campaigning groups in the South simply continued, as they were independent entities already. These included Jubilee South that brought together several smaller groupings, Jubilee USA and the German-based Erlassjahr.de.

In the UK the campaigning work on debt continued under three new organisations. There was a short-term campaign, led by Adrian Lovett (the Deputy Director) focusing on the Genoa G8 in 2001 under the name Drop the Debt. This aimed to maximise pressure on the G7 before and during the Genoa summit in Italy for July 2001. There were strong indications that the Italian government wanted to bring forward a new initiative on debt. The debt cancellation campaigning used new banners but there was the same spirit as campaigners descended on the city.

But the battle is still not over. Some debt has been cancelled; but vast mountains of debt remain. At present the world's poorest countries are paying on average about 40% of Government revenues in debt servicing – a daily total of about $60 million. For every £1 given in development aid, £13 is claimed back from the poorest countries in debt repayments. Promises of cancellation have been made, but have yet to be fully realised. Of the 52 countries for which Jubilee 2000 requested debt relief (totalling $360 billion), only 23 have so far benefited. Thousands of children still die each day because of debt. Though the Jubilee 2000 Coalition officially ended at the end of December 2000, the work continues. Campaigners are travelling to Genoa, Italy this weekend to again raise their demands with the G8 for full debt relief.

Drop the Debt, 2001

Ann's work continued under the umbrella of the New Economics Foundation as Jubilee Plus, carrying out significant work on research, monitoring and international liaison on the issues of debt, and wider issues of international financial flows and institutions, and now simply providing an information resource.

And the main ongoing work, then and now, was taken up by a new organization that took the name of Jubilee Debt Campaign. It was launched on Saturday, 24th March 2001 and Bill and Martin were both elected to join the board. Their first major project was to work alongside Drop the Debt targeting the G7 Summit in Genoa. Their key aim was to secure 100% debt cancellation from multilateral lenders (the IMF and World Bank) to match the 100% bilateral debt cancellation already agreed by most G7 governments.

During the final months of 2000 and in early 2001, I took a leading and highly vociferous part in calling for the re-launch of the Jubilee Campaign in the new millennium – in the teeth of opposition from some of the leading players in Jubilee 2000! We won that one and the campaign was reborn as 'Jubilee Debt Campaign' in March 2001, at which time I was elected onto the Board of Trustees, a position I have held until the present time.

David Golding
Newcastle University and Trustee of Jubilee Debt Campaign

Rickshaw freedom fighters heading for Genoa, 2001

The issue of debt was again a key focus in 2005 as part of the Make Poverty History campaign. At the G8 summit hosted by the UK in Gleneagles, an astonishing 225,000 people gathered as part of a mass rally which encircled Edinburgh.

155

Just before this summit, following a meeting of G8 finance ministers, Gordon Brown announced that the G8 members – the world's eight wealthiest countries – would cancel $55 billion (£30 billion) of Third World debt. The IMF and World Bank released the details of this Multilateral Debt Relief Initiative (MDRI) two months later, working through HIPC and offering debt cancellation for countries that met the HIPC criteria. This was a really significant step and was the first plan that suggested a lasting resolution of the 'HIPC problem'. MDRI cancelled $40 billion (£22 billion) of debt immediately for 18 of the world's poorest countries already undergoing the HIPC process. Another $11 billion from a further nine countries would be written off twelve to eighteen months later.

One additional outcome of the Gleneagles summit was the commitment, by all UK political parties, to maintain the aid target of spending 0.7% of national income on aid – an agreement that still stands today – *just* (though it has become somewhat debatable as to what constitutes aid and what constitutes military spending).

List of HIPC eligible countries (as of September 2016)[8]

Countries that have reached Completion Point (36)

Afghanistan	Comoros	Guinea-Bissau
Benin	Republic of Congo	Guyana
Bolivia	Democratic Republic of Congo	Haiti
Burkina Faso		Honduras
Burundi	Côte d'Ivoire	Liberia
Cameroon	Ethiopia	Madagascar
Central African Republic	The Gambia	Malawi
	Ghana	Mali
Chad	Guinea	

---

[8] IMF Factsheet September 2016,
www.imf.org/en/About/Factsheets/Sheets/2016/08/01/16/11/Debt-Relief-Under-the-Heavily-Indebted-Poor-Countries-Initiative

Mauritania	Rwanda	Tanzania
Mozambique	São Tomé & Príncipe	Togo
Nicaragua	Senegal	Uganda
Niger	Sierra Leone	Zambia

Eligible Countries Pre-Decision-Point (3)

Eritrea	Somalia	Sudan

By the end of 2016 international loans totalling more than US$ 96 billion have been cancelled for the 36 countries that have reached the completion point for HIPC. This has saved these 36 countries approximately $3 billion annually in interest payments, which under HIPC terms has to be invested in health, education, clean water and other social services.

Children hand over their piggy banks to bemused Treasury officials.

Piggy banks given to Treasury officials

157

CHAPTER TWENTY

Some Final Reflections

Why write up these reflections now – so many years later? Jubilee 2000 came at a very pressured time of life for me – with three teenage children, work with Tearfund that I loved and whilst beginning a part-time Ph.D. on a topic that fascinated me: how agricultural information is shared informally at grass roots levels around the world. Fitting in all the work for Jubilee 2000 was a massive pressure. Once I stepped down in 1998, my time was immediately filled by catching up with my somewhat neglected Ph.D. The 'vision' was not something I wanted to publicise or dwell on. We moved home later that year to Shropshire where it was very refreshing not to be immediately labelled with 'Jubilee 2000'.

Another consideration was my awareness of other people's situations. Founder members Bill and Martin struggled considerably with the loss of influence of 'their baby' as the coalition took off. They were well aware that titles given them were honorary and allowed them far less input than they would have liked in the later years of the campaign. I respected their self-esteem too much to want to be seen to dilute in any way their amazing commitment and passion for seeing Third World debt cancelled. My story had had a different beginning which I hadn't wanted to share widely at the time, and so it was easier to continue the silence.

But now the 20th anniversary of the Birmingham chain is fast approaching (May 2018) – an anniversary that will hopefully be marked in some meaningful way. In addition, Jubilee 2000 and the coalition that formed around it are still talked about, comparisons are still made, and there are a lot of inaccurate summaries circulating of how the campaigning all began. I'm sure parts of this 'inside story' will still be of interest to all those wonderful people who got caught up in the issue at the time and will stimulate their own recollections. For many thousands Jubilee 2000 brought about an awakening of social justice and an awareness of the power of advocacy and campaigning on behalf of others

And overwhelmingly I had a sudden sense that the time was simply right to put all this down on paper. I no longer had the sense of embarrassment regarding the 'vision'! I've been surprised by just how enjoyable and fascinating the process of piecing together the memories has proved. However, I do sincerely regret not writing a diary, which would have been such a help in sorting through the boxes of papers!

Jonathan Glennie wrote an article in *The Guardian*, April 2011 reflecting back:

The Jubilee movement is special to millions of people who cut their campaigning teeth on it and learned from its success.

There are many reasons why the Jubilee movement is so special for so many of us. First, it worked. For many years the economists of the World Bank and the British treasury had told us that debt simply could not be cancelled. It was a moral hazard. There were rules.

But they hadn't reckoned on the moral power of the human chain around the Birmingham G8 in 1998, chanting for debt cancellation – famously audible to the negotiators in their conference rooms. When debt cancellation finally became a reality for some countries, it led to increased spending on health and education, saving and improving millions of lives.

…When the leaflets started going out, when the talks started to be given in church halls and scout huts, the British people were shocked to learn about the injustice that their country was inflicting on the world's poorest people. They got it. It was the first time UK charities, working with others across the world, had gathered en masse to fight against global unfairness. It was a paradigm shift.

…At a time when mass campaigns on global injustice seem like ancient history as rich countries themselves struggle with deep

> *financial problems, we should remember the great moments in the*
> *history of the Jubilee debt movement. We need to find that spirit*
> *again from somewhere. What will be the next Jubilee 2000?*

In hindsight I often still wonder, why me? Why was I called to help birth this campaign? Certainly not because I am in any way anything other than a 'middle of the road' Christian believer – rarely given to particular insights or devotion. But when God speaks, I certainly do take him very seriously.

Retrospection is always helpful and as I look back, lots of reasons fall into place. I was someone who was passionate about the injustices of this world (having worked in PNG, Ethiopia and Kenya) and was already involved in the development world and aid circles (and the Tearfund link proved a pretty key one). My working life focuses on the need for clear communications, and on sharing practical information that is easy to implement – and that certainly helped hugely in wading through the intricacies of Third World debt. I also had some pretty amazing friends – people who provided start-up funds, logos, inspiration, ideas, design inputs – who all had a massive input.

The links with Hull and the anti-slavery movement also all brought great resonance and useful links. Over the years, I have learnt that I can be an effective facilitator and am pretty good at making things happen if I put my mind to it. Basically, I believe it all came about simply because I happened to be a useful person with a lot of relevant links at that particular time. God just put all those to use.

Ultimately, we never achieved in full the vision of Jubilee 2000 – a matter of enormous regret. We realised too late how little public support there was in the USA, a fact that was to prove somewhat crucial. Despite Clinton's earlier commitments on debt cancellation in 1999, his focus shifted. By early 2000 we knew that half of the members of the G8 were with us. But a key change came during 2000 as Clinton turned his focus onto Israel and the urgent need to intervene in the struggling Middle East peace process.

So the celebration was not as God's vision had indicated – which was all our loss. Could we have done more? That's hard to envisage, particularly given the exhaustion of the office staff at the end of 2000.

However, together the Jubilee 2000 coalition did change the thinking around Third World debt completely.

Instead of a complex quagmire of negotiations and debt reduction papers, we had provided a clear and acceptable solution through requesting a one-off cancellation of unpayable debt. We had changed the thinking around the debt issue so that no longer were there questions about whether debt should be cancelled, but instead it simply became a matter of when this would happen. Reading reports from organisations such as the Department for International Development (DFID), it is really encouraging to see how their wording changes from 1999 onwards.

Debt cancellation continues to be outworked by the sterling work of Jubilee Debt Campaign, also now taking under its wing current day issues of debt within Europe.

For many of our supporters, particularly within the churches, Jubilee 2000 provided their first 'taste' of advocacy work. Many have continued this involvement with a myriad of other campaigns. The Make Poverty History campaign in 2005, culminating with a massive gathering and march of 250,000 people in Edinburgh at the time of the G8 meeting in Gleneagles, was a direct beneficiary of the passion and support for advocacy work for global justice awakened by Jubilee 2000.

Jubilee Debt Campaign had to fight very hard to get debt onto the Make Poverty History agenda, but that turned out to be just where Make Poverty History had the most impact, with a new deal on debt which aimed to wipe out much of the multilateral debt sock for countries that had successfully gone through the HIPC process – an additional $50 billion in debt cancellation for 41 countries.

Stephen Rand
Stephen Rand was Communications Director
then Prayer and Campaigns Director for Tearfund
and Co-chair of Jubilee Debt Campaign

No longer are advocacy and campaigning work regarded as somehow not relevant for Christians. Indeed, Christian agencies have taken forward that agenda with flair, regarding the equipping of their supporters to engage in practical action as a fundamental focus.

161

Why not you?

I hope that a sense comes through of the way in which God drew together a unique grouping of ordinary people to really make a difference. I am convinced that God still intervenes and prompts ordinary people in our needy world. So please don't ignore your own heart if you sense God's prompting. He rarely moves in straightforward ways and still likes to use the 'nobodies' of this world. Yes, of course, do check ideas and inspiration out very carefully with others. If appropriate, maybe consider using the biblically based principal of fleeces. Stifling God's voice is a well-practised art, but fortunately, there are plenty of people who still respond and through whom God can and does achieve some amazing things.

Further Reading and References

Barrett, Marlene (2000) Editor; *The world will never be the same again;* Jubilee 2000 Coalition and World Vision

Bono, 1999. 'World Debt Angers Me.' *The Guardian;* Tuesday, February16th.

Dent, Martin (1990); *Why We Are Founding Jubilee 2000;* unpublished paper, 10th February 1990

Dent, Martin and Peters, Bill (1999); *The Crisis of Poverty and Debt in the Third World;* Aldershot: Ashgate

Evans, Alex and Gower, Richard (2015); *The Restorative Economy: Completing Our Unfinished Millennium Jubilee;* Tearfund.

Freer, Matthew D. (1999); *Issues of NGO Advocacy, Public Campaign Action and Perceptions of Cancellation of Unpayable Poor Country Debt; A Case Study of Jubilee 2000;* Dept. of Geography, Royal Holloway University of London.

George, Susan (1992); *The Debt Boomerang. How Third World Debt Harms Us All;* Pluto Press.

Hanson, Ingrid (1996); *The Debt Cutter's Handbook;* Jubilee, 2000

Hanson, Ingrid and Travis (1999); *Breaking the Chains;* Jubilee 2000 Coalition

Jubilee Debt Campaign (2008); *Unfinished business: Ten years of dropping the debt*

Peters, Bill (1994); 'Jubilee 2000', *Journal of Modern African Studies* 32; 4 pp 699-700

Randle, Michael (2004); *Jubilee 2000; the challenge of coalition campaigning;* Centre for the Study of Forgiveness and Reconciliation, Coventry University

Selby, Peter (1997); *Grace and Mortgage: Language of Faith and the Debt of the World;* Darton, Longman & Todd Ltd.

What Shall I Read Next?

Publisher's Recommendations

Hope in the Main Street
Rob Cotton
ISBN 978-1-78815-639-4

Rev. Rob Cotton demonstrates how our churches can engage with the community around, building relationships that enable social action, presenting the teachings of the Bible in ways that contemporary audiences can relate to and presenting Christianity as genuine good news. Rob has led a number of churches, as well as being Senior Campaign Manager at Bible Society and on the leadership teams for national campaigns such as Hope 08, Biblefresh and The 2011 Trust (celebrating the 400th anniversary of the King James Bible). From the humorous to the heartbreaking, these stories from his years of ministry will equip you, encourage you and challenge you to bring 'hope on the main street'.

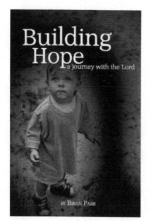

Building Hope
Bryan Parr
ISBN 978-1-907509-13-1

Bryan Parr had been a Christian for many years and was now retired. But one day, as he went through the motions of his Sunday church service, he found himself asking, "Is this all there is to Christianity?" His question led him to find ways to bring hope to the neediest in eastern Europe, using his building skills to create orphanages and work on other vital projects – to bring good news to the poor.

These books are available from all good bookshops
and from the publisher:

www.onwardsandupwards.org